MYSTERIOUS KEMET

BOOK - II

SEDUCTION & CONSPIRACY IN ANCIENT EGYPT

S. R. ANAND

MYSTERIOUS KEMET
BOOK II

First published in 2017.

ISBN-10: 1521161593
ISBN-13: 978-1521161593

Cover Art: Shafali

2 0 1 7 0 4 2 6 1 0

To my readers.

ACKNOWLEDGMENTS

My heartfelt thanks to:

My friend Nancy for her invaluable feedback on this book, and for her beautiful friendship.

My mom for being my first teacher and nurturing my love for reading and telling stories. Though she's no longer with us, I know that her blessings will always light my way.

My dad for bringing me my first storybooks and letting me be myself.

My angel fur-kid Oorvi for filling our lives with a million happy moments. Had she not come into my life, I wouldn't have written my first book.

David Farland for his awesome newsletter and articles, and for the email that I had received from him three years ago.

Sid and Rita for their suggestions, which helped enrich the stories.

Bobby, my sweetheart and my soulmate, for his break-my-heart reviews and his unending patience and loving care. Without his unconditional support, my stories wouldn't have reached my readers.

Thank you.

The Stories

I
THE RIVER BRIDE
~ | PRE-DYNASTIC PERIOD | ~

In pre-dynastic Egypt, the androgynous river god Hapi awaits his bride. As the greed of one woman collides with the desire of another, a young man tries to save the girl he loves from a lottery that has all odds stacked against her. In the tumult that ensues, a middle-aged priestess, who is caught in the conspiracy unawares, must either overcome her revulsion for a dwarf's overtures or face certain death.

II
THE NECROPHILE'S RING
~ | NEW KINGDOM | ~

The city of Thinis is undivided in its opinion. The necrophile must burn for his depravity. As the accused waits for his sentence to be carried out, three women – a love-priestess, a troubled wife, and the young daughter of an embalmer, struggle to discover the truth and find a proof that could save an innocent life.

III

THE BREWERESS OF OMBO
~ | PTOLEMAIC EGYPT | ~

Caught in a complex web of Roman politics, royal fratricide, and two fruitless incestuous marriages, Cleopatra must use her charisma and ingenuity to find a way to follow her secret dream, but despite all her efforts, she should pay for it with a crown and the life of a loved one.

IV

THE SPINNER OF DREAMS
~ | NEW KINGDOM – END OF AMARNA PERIOD | ~

As Pharaoh Ay lies dying, his son Nakhtmin, the crown prince of Egypt, must either accept the crown and rule Egypt, or change Egypt's destiny by exacting an unexpected revenge from his ambitious, brilliant, but homophobic father who killed not only Nakhtmin's lover, but also his love for life.

V

THE BLUE LILY

Like the other chosen ones, Mentu is destined to follow his King into the afterlife. Following the death of the King, he must place his trust in Khuit, his concubine of ten years who was once a wharf-wench. For both Mentu and Khuit, it is their only chance at life, but what is life for one, is death for the other, unless fate intervenes.

Story One

THE RIVER BRIDE

~ | Pre-dynastic Period | ~

THE RIVER BRIDE

The priestess sat upon the packed mud floor of her bedchamber, her shoulders shaking, her massive chest heaving under her labored breathing, and her eyes swollen from hours of crying.

This would be her last night in this world. She was completely clueless about how it had all come about, but she knew for sure that there were many in the city who would be happy to drown her.

"How did this happen?" she sobbed, tears trickling down her face.

Behind her, the door cracked open and threw streak of light upon the floor in front of her. Then a shadow filled the lighted space.

She raised her tear-stricken face and saw the short, stubby figure of the Holy Dwarf.

"It doesn't matter how. We are the priests and our word cannot be questioned. We must help *Hapi* claim his own bride," the dwarf came in and stopped close to where she was sitting.

"Is it even possible?" she whimpered.

"Did you not hear my pronouncement? The river god wishes to claim his own bride this year."

The priestess looked up. The Holy Dwarf's features were hidden in the shadows but the light that shone through the door behind him outlined his face.

He didn't look ugly anymore.

In him she saw a god.

He was truly the incarnation of the god Bes.

〰 ᑉᑉᑉ 〰

A month ago, before the end of *Shemu,* the preparations for *Hapi's* appeasement had begun in the city of Naqada, and the biggest center of attraction in the city was the temple complex.

The complex was beautiful. The front yard that was enclosed by a wall of sunbaked bricks was a large area paved with sandstone, and around it stood several temples. Upon entering the yard, right ahead was the temple of *Ra,* which was flanked on the left by the temple of *Hapi.* At its right stood the shrine of *Isis.* Then there were the temples of other minor deities too, but these three were the more important ones for they belonged to the gods that were responsible for the prosperity of the people of Egypt.

The sun god *Ra* went around the earth, changing his form, brightening the land with light and defining the cycle of life. *Isis,* the mother goddess was responsible for making the women of Egypt fertile. She, who could give birth to *Horus* by coupling with her dead brother, obviously was the one whose blessings were needed by every woman of childbearing age. And then, there was *Hapi* - male in his attributes of strength and virility, and female in her virtues of fertility and nurture. *Hapi* controlled the annual flooding of the Nile, ensuring that the land remained fertile and the people of Egypt didn't go hungry.

When the season of *Shemu* ended, *Hapi* became the cynosure of the land of Egypt. In all the settlements, be they villages, towns, or cities, *Hapi*'s temples turned into the busiest places of worship, for if *Hapi* wasn't propitiated, come the season of *Akhet*, Nile's inundation would leave something to be desired. It would either rise too high and flood its banks, leaving disease and death in its wake; or remain too low and cause famine.

Quite like in all other cities, in Naqada too, worshippers were beginning to throng the temple of *Hapi*. Outside the complex, the amulet sellers were doing brisk business. Clay figurines of a bearded *Hapi* with large pendulous breasts were the biggest sellers at this time of the year.

Today, the priests of *Hapi* would leave the temple complex in a procession, singing the praises of the hermaphrodite god, carrying with them the urn of *Hapi*'s bride. The parents of every girl who had been blessed with her first blood that year would speak their own names along with their daughter's, and the temple-scribe would then etch the information on a clay tablet and drop the tablet into the urn of *Hapi*'s bride.

In the house of Meriptah, the richest trader in Naqada, there was one such young girl. Neri had just turned thirteen, and the rich red elixir of life had for the first time flown upon her young thighs, just five months ago. Less than a month before she had flowered, her father had died. He was returning from the delta where he went twice a year to buy his merchandize, and had been killed by a gang of robbers in the eastern *wadis*.

Neri sat upon the edge of her bed, deafened by the silence in the house. Her friend who lived in the neighboring house too was going to have her name etched for the lottery this year. Her friend's parents had been going to the temple everyday, praying to all the Gods and leaving them the gifts they could afford, so that their daughter may be spared – for the name that the Holy Dwarf would finally draw from the urn, would mark the girl who would become the river-bride this year.

Neri imagined how different her life would have been had her father been alive. He would've gone to every temple and shrine, appeased all the gods, however insignificant they might have been, and bribed them with linen and pottery so that they convinced *Hapi* to spare his daughter. Meriptah, her father, had been fretting over his daughter's fate for the last three years. Sometimes Neri wondered if her father's prayers were keeping her blood from flowing, for soon after her father's death, her flower had blossomed.

She now lived with her stepmother Mutret, the woman her father married after Neri's mother had died giving birth to her younger brother. Meriptah had married Mutret when Neri was five and her brother was two. Her brother didn't survive his first year under Mutret's care, and Mutret herself bore no children – and so now, after her father's death, Neri and Mutret were the only ones living in the house.

Neri rose from her bed and went to her *ankh*-table, which had once belonged to her mother. Standing there, her eyes were drawn to her reflection. She was thin, with a long neck, and eyes so big that they didn't look like they belonged on her face. Her father always told her that she was pretty, but then every father thought that his daughter's was the sweetest face in the world.

She looked away from her reflection. It brought her no happiness.

The short-legged sled-table that had an *ankh*-shaped mirror attached to it had a drawer that could be pulled out. Inside the drawer, along with her shell comb, galena stick, and a small ivory jewelry box that had a beautiful and detailed carving of the winged *Isis*, there was a small roll of papyrus. Neri pulled the drawer out, removed the papyrus, and unrolled it upon the surface of the table. Inside was an image of her father. He was a tall and handsome man with a ready smile. When her father had died, Temnet, her childhood friend, had drawn his face for her, so that she could still look upon him, even though he had now gone to the afterlife.

Tears came unbidden and rolled down her cheeks. She raised her eyes from the papyrus and looked at her reflection in the once polished brass surface of the mirror, which was now stained with verdigris. The girl that stared back at her looked like nothing much. Just a reedy thing with huge green eyes – not fit to be anyone's bride, let alone *Hapi's*. She thought she should polish the mirror, but then she remembered the lottery and decided to wait.

Another month, she thought, *and I will be gone. With flowers in my hair and bathed in fragrances, I'll be sent into Hapi's embrace, for there is nobody in this world who would pray to the gods for me.*

As *Ra* rode into the sky to shine upon Naqada with all its summer fury, and the priests made their way through the streets of the city, Neri heard the lutes play and the drums beat.

With each beat of the drum, she heard her name being called out.

Neri…Neri…Neri,
Dum…deedum…deedum.

Her hands flew to her ears making the scroll with her father's image fall into her lap as she tried to drown the sounds that poured through the window and flooded her soul, drowning her, making her gasp for breath…*as she would*

when flung into Hapi's embrace.

᠕᠕᠕ ۝۝۝ ᠕᠕᠕

Aeti ran through the crowded streets of Naqada,

bumping into the melon-seller, scattering his melons and sending them rolling; jumping over the amulet-hawker's wares; and crashing into the women who were out in the streets haggling with the vendors.

With only two days left before the ceremony, visitors were already beginning to arrive. They came from nearby towns and villages – men, women, and children – some even brought their goats along. The markets that weren't exactly quiet the rest of the year, had turned into deafeningly noisy places, glittering with wares that the merchants were keeping aside for this occasion. The sounds of haggling and bartering filled the atmosphere, the same as the smells of the porters' sweat mixed with the perfumes worn by the ladies who traveled in curtained litters and palanquins.

"Has *Nekhbet* eaten your eyes, boy?" screamed a middle-aged matron who went sprawling upon a heap of pomegranates, as he bumped into her.

He apologized without breaking his pace, and ignored her insult. *Nekhbet*, the vulture god was responsible for the well-being of half the Egypt, and Aeti was sure, he wouldn't waste his time picking out a boy's eyes. At this time, Aeti's own mission was more important than the harridan's bruised ego.

It was a matter of life and death.

He didn't know how they could reverse what had already happened the night before, but he knew that Temnet was an imaginative and inventive individual, and if Aeti told him the facts, he would come up with something.

Aeti too was studying to be a scribe, the same as Temnet, and among the many skills a scribe acquired was the ability to differentiate between the important and the mundane, and without a speck of doubt, what Aeti had learned last night was something that he couldn't have ignored.

Temnet's father owned some of the most fertile land on the banks of Nile, and while Temnet loved to paint and wanted to become either an artist or a scribe, it was as clear as the after-noon sky that he would eventually follow his father's footsteps. But right now, Temnet was young. Barely seventeen. He and Aeti had become friends in their hieroglyph drawing class.

Hieroglyphs were drawings that were etched on clay tablets to record information and events by substituting pictures for sounds and objects. They had been around only for about a hundred years, and now they had become so entrenched in every aspect of administration that it was difficult to imagine life without them. Being a scribe required the knowledge of all the hieroglyphs and an ability to etch them in clay clearly, and Temnet was very good at both.

Of course there was a big difference between their situations. Temnet was the son of a rich merchant and so he came to the temple complex only to learn, while Aeti who was an orphan with nobody to finance his studies, lived, worked, and studied in the complex. In return for food and shelter, he did odd jobs such as cleaning the rooms of the priests and running their chores.

"Temnet," he shouted, running up the steps of his friend's house two at a time.

The fool might be still asleep, he thought, running across the yard as rivulets of sweat streamed down his temples.

"Temnet," he shouted again, cupping his hands around his mouth to throw his voice toward Temnet's window.

Finally, his friend's head appeared in the frame of the window.

"I would have met you at the temple anyway," Temnet grumbled but waved his friend up to his room.

Aeti knew the way to his friend's room, which was double the size of his own at the temple complex, and unlike his, was richly decorated. Temnet had painted his walls himself and he had a bed with a mattress covered with pure white linen. He also had a table upon which he kept his scrolls and pens, and a couple of stools to sit upon. Aeti perched himself upon one of the stools.

"Water?" Temnet held out the water jar for him. Aeti snatched it from Temnet and drank greedily.

"You ran all the way?" Temnet asked him.

"Not all the way, but most of it. I don't own a donkey like you do," Aeti answered, splashing the last of the water upon his face.

"What couldn't have waited until we met this afternoon?" Temnet asked in a concerned voice.

Temnet knew that the priests and the acolytes lived in a monastery attached to the temple complex and in the nights they slept on the terrace. Aeti told him that hadn't been able to sleep because his stomach had been churning and groaning under the influence of something that he had eaten that afternoon. So he had gone out of the compound to relieve himself. When he was returning, Aeti had heard the sounds. Curious, he had stayed to check.

"What sounds?" Temnet asked.

"I couldn't make them out at first, but then I followed them and realized that they were coming from Rahop's chamber," Aeti explained.

"Rahop was sleeping inside his room? In this terrible heat?" Temnet asked, surprised.

Rahop was one of the junior priests. He was about twenty-five, and he was one of the assistants of the priest of *Amun*.

"Sleeping? Who said that he was sleeping?" Aeti smirked.

Sitting there in Temnet's room, everything appeared incredibly dreamlike, but Aeti knew that it wasn't. *Whatever had happened the previous night was everything that he had been taught to consider a sin.*

Aeti had found that Rahop's reed curtains upon his door

and window were both lowered. The heat was oppressive and the fact that Rahop had decided to shut himself inside his room for the night was enough to make Aeti curious. He had tiptoed to the reed curtain on the window and peeked inside. Rahop's window in the opposite wall was open. It was a full moon night and his bed flushed to the wall under the open window, was awash with a silvery glow.

Upon the bed, he saw them. Entwined, like a pair of cobras. Her fair skin gleamed silvery against his darker flesh. The scene inside Rahop's room was deliciously shocking for Aeti. The priests were sworn to celibacy, but he had heard rumors that some priests nurtured their carnal interests despite their vows – and yet, copulation within the temple premises was unprecedented, and even considered blasphemous.

The improbability of the situation along with its apparent immorality had made the scene in front of Aeti all the more thrilling for him. He was sixteen and just beginning to experiment with both religion and sex. He might leave one for the other, he knew, but that day was still far away.

Standing outside Rahop's window, his eyes riveted to the scene that lit up upon the bed, he felt himself rise. The woman was on top of Rahop. Her fair skin reflected the moonlight as her body's contours filled his view. She sat astride him, massaging Rahop's stele, making it rise so that its head glistened in the same moonlight that trailed across her soft big breasts and bounced down her round belly. Then she raised her body to devour Rahop's willing member, excited at the prospect of finding itself ensconced within her softness. When she lowered herself upon him, she moaned drawing deep throaty groans from Rahop.

Aeti watched spellbound, as the woman rode Rahop; their silhouettes slick with perspiration, shining, glistening, bouncing, and crashing into each other. Aeti felt his knees buckling. He didn't want to miss any of it, and so he tried to tear his attention away from his own little monster tensing and demanding succor. Aeti had always loved women who looked like the woman inside. He had been with a few but his experiences were severely limited by his means. The love-priestesses that he could afford weren't as soft and clean as the woman who was joined with Rahop inside the room. There was something about rich and inaccessible women – women who wore wigs and traveled in litters, which made them a lot more attractive than the streetwalkers.

Though he couldn't see her face clearly, her presence here, in the middle of the night, and the jewels that glittered upon her fingers, arms, and ankles, told him that she was rich.

He watched their coupling bodies as they strained and pulled at each other. The squishing sounds of their perspiring bodies meeting each-other; the low guttural noises of pleasure escaping their throats; and the little moans made by the woman when Rahop's hands clutched at her bounteous breasts that bounced to imitate the rhythm of her strokes; they all made Aeti's heart race up and thump against his ribs. Fascinated, he watched the flesh of the woman's full thighs leap and jump, as their lovemaking accelerated toward climax.

The shudders came in waves, inundating the couple as the clawed at each other's bodies, Rahop stretching against the bed, and the woman arching away from him – pearly drops of sweat falling off her nipples into the tiny nest of hair below.

Aeti suddenly realized the peril of his situation. Soon the mist of their passionate lovemaking would recede, leaving their senses clear. He dropped the reed curtain as softly as he could, and conscious of his own heavy breathing, he slowly drew himself into the shadows. He could have left, but he didn't, because his curiosity had grown.

He wanted to see who the woman was.

"Did you find out?" Temnet asked, his eyes shining in anticipation.

"I did," Aeti replied. He had waited in the shadows, subtly conscious and regretful of his own excitement fading, until the reed-curtain that hung from Rahop's door was lifted and the woman had stepped out.

With a shock, Aeti had recognized her.

But he had run across half the city to meet and warn his friend, not because he had recognized the woman, but because he had stayed hidden in the shadows and witnessed the events that had followed her departure.

ᴡᴡ ᑫᑫᑫ ᴡᴡ

The house adjacent to Temnet's had once belonged to Meriptah. Now it belonged to Neri and her stepmother Mutret. While Temnet and Aeti sat talking in Temnet's house, Neri's stepmother Mutret stomped toward the girl's room.

"Your father left us destitute," Mutret grumbled as she entered Neri's room and rolled up the reed curtain on her window. Light flooded in. Neri's was a small room, neat, with an *ankh*-table near the window.

Neri hadn't slept the previous night, or the night before. She hadn't been sleeping well since the names were collected. Her friend Temnet had once told her that only the worries of future could keep a person awake in the night. He was right, for never before her father's death, had Neri lost her sleep. She had first been plagued with endless stargazing when her father had died, but in time she had learned to accept that she was meant to live alone. Now, once again, she had found herself dreading her future.

The Priestess of *Hapi* had announced that the urn had three hundred and nineteen names, and Neri knew well that one of those names was hers. With both her parents dead, there was not a soul in the world who would pray for her wellbeing, and everyone knew that gods didn't help you for nothing. Temnet had brought her an amulet though, but he wasn't related to her by blood, which meant that his prayers would never be as potent as those offered on behalf of the other girls, and yet she had worn that amulet around her neck and gone to bed, clutching it, praying to the gods. She didn't want to die. They said that becoming the river-bride wasn't dying; it was marrying *Hapi*. But she didn't want to marry that blue-skinned androgynous god either. He was pot-bellied and he had the jugs of an old woman. Future, to her, looked bleak, and whenever she did end up falling into a fitful sleep, she dreamed of drowning.

"I hope the dwarf picks your name," her stepmother said, looking out of the window at nothing in particular.

Neri and Mutret had a relationship that was built on honesty and transparency. Mutret made no bones about how much she hated her stepdaughter, and Neri did nothing to hide her indifference for her stepmother.

"Why?" Neri asked, her eyes wide and sad. When Neri looked at herself in her polished brass mirror, she couldn't see what Mutret saw, or she may have understood at least one of the reasons that made her stepmother hate her.

Mutret saw in her a lovely young woman with big eyes that curved on the outside. Even without a touch of malachite, her eyes were bewitching, for the soft green of her irises was hypnotic. Neri's skin was clear and unblemished, and it was the color of wheat with a touch of rose. Her oval face sat upon a long, graceful neck, and her hair shone black as a raven's wings. With a body supple as a willow stem, she was the antithesis of her stepmother.

Mutret herself had just climbed to the other side of thirty and her body was full in a provocatively curvaceous manner. Her complexion was only slightly darker than her step-daughter's but her hair was still the same color as Neri's. She was still too young for her hair to turn gray. What made Mutret's face forbidding and stern and rendered it plain, were her dark and suspicious brown eyes, which set deep under her taut eyebrows complemented her constant frown.

"Why? Oh, well. The biggest reason is that I cannot stand you," Mutret replied to Neri's question.

"Nobody is praying for me, so there's a strong chance that my name would be picked," Neri said, her voice catching in her throat, as her hand subconsciously found the amulet that Temnet had brought her.

Mutret caught Neri's action from the corner of her eye.

"What is it?" she enquired.

"Nothing," Neri parried.

"So you've been offering prayers on your own," her stepmother laughed raucously.

Neri looked at Mutret and thought how different her life would have been had her own mother been alive.

Neri drew a long sharp breath, and waited for Mutret to leave the room. At the door, Mutret turned and looked into Neri's eyes.

"You have nobody and nothing to live for," she said.

Neri felt hatred swell in her heart and for the first time in her life, she found her courage.

"You are wrong. I have someone to live for," she replied, her eyes blazing anger, "but you have nobody to call your own. It doesn't matter how many people pray for me. A single prayer offered with love and hope can reach the gods, and I have someone who has prayed for me."

Mutret retorted sharply. "Oh, and who is that?" She then stood drumming her fingers upon the windowsill, staring Neri down. "Let me guess. That girl who is your friend, but she has her name in the urn too, so it cannot be her. Most others don't even know that you are alive. That aunt of yours, the one who lives in Thinis, would have to think hard to remember your name. She hasn't seen you in years. Who is it then?"

Neri sat silent and defiant, her eyes raining fire, but her lips stitched close to control her fury. Her indifference for her stepmother was already turning into anger.

Mutret continued.

"It can then only be that fool Temnet. I've seen the way he looks at you," she said, chewing each word as she stared hard at Neri.

"Tell me something, girl. Have you been with him?"

Neri didn't reply.

Mutret shook her head slightly, screwing up her eyes. "You won't tell, but if the Holy Dwarf picks your name, then your husband *Hapi* would know. He would know, and how would he react if he discovered that his bride wasn't a virgin?" She came closer to Neri and jerked her chin up. "How would he feel then?"

Neri stayed defiant, digging her chin into her stepmother's palm.

The lines of Mutret's face became harder and straighter.

"It doesn't matter, does it? You'll be gone from this world and this house, and that is the only thing that matters."

Neri pushed away her stepmother's hand and stood up.

"Don't be so sure," she said, looking into Mutret's eyes. "There are three hundred and nineteen names in the urn."

Mutret let out a shrill laugh.

"And everyone has their family praying for them. Your chances are bleak, my dear," she threw Neri a parting shot and left the room.

Clutching her amulet and overtaken with a mixture of anger, fear, and grief, Neri screamed.

"You are a horrible woman, Mutret! When you reach the world beyond, you will forget the directions. When your heart is weighed, the scale of *Anubis* will break, and *Ammit* will devour it with relish. Heartless, you'll wander in darkness forever."

Neri's voice wrapped itself around Mutret, and tightened around her ribs like a cobra's embrace, making her gasp for breath.

It won't matter. After tomorrow, all this won't matter, Mutret thought frantically, as she tried to control her racing heart.

∿∿ ◊◊◊ ∿∿

"That's impossible," thundered Temnet.

Aeti got up, loosened his pouch from his belt, and rummaged within. His fingers found what he was looking for and he drew it out.

"Find its pair," he threw an earring upon Temnet's bed.

It was a tiny baked clay figurine in blue set between two red beads. A thin gold wire ran through the beads and the figurine, and was fashioned into a hook at its top end.

"I recognize it," Temnet said, picking it up. He had seen it in the ears of Neri's stepmother Mutret.

"When I went in to clean his room this morning, I found it under Rahop's bed," Aeti said, pointing to the earring. "I picked it up. Though it isn't much of a proof, but I thought you might recognize it, and so I brought it along. And here's one of the tablets that Rahop replaced the ones in the urn with," he dipped his hand into his pouch once again and produced a baked clay tablet.

Temnet sank upon the edge of his bed, holding the tablet in his hand. He had been praying to the gods every day and he had convinced himself that his prayers would be answered. He loved her. Each day, he went to bed dreaming of her. She was his first thought of the day, and his last – and she filled every empty moment in between.

He held the clay tablet with both hands, between his

thumbs and his forefingers, wanting to twist and break it – but breaking it won't change anything.

"He replaced all of them with this?" he asked, his voice broken and distant. His world would be nothing without Neri. She was meant to be his bride not Hapi's.

"All three hundred and nineteen of them," Aeti confirmed. "I removed one, so the urn still contains three hundred and eighteen clay tablets with Neri's name upon them. When the Holy Dwarf dips his hand into the urn in front of half of Naqada, he won't draw any name other than Neri's."

Temnet listened to his friend, allowing himself to absorb the shock. He had no recollection of that exact moment when he had fallen in love. The little girl in the neighborhood had grown into a lovely young woman, and she had danced straight into his heart, sometime during the last year. They had been meeting secretly, talking about themselves, because both wanted to know everything they could about the other. Her questions had told him that his love was reciprocated, and he was sure that if he told his father that he wanted to marry Neri, he would happily agree – not for any love toward the young orphan, but because she was his friend's daughter and now also the owner of half her father's property. Temnet's father was a shrewd businessman and he never passed up a profitable opportunity.

When he had learned that her name had gone into the urn, he had fretted, but then Aeti had asked him to buy an amulet of *Hapi* and get it blessed by the priests of all the temples in the complex. Aeti had told him that his amulet would protect Neri as will his love for her. He had tied the amulet around her neck, and told her that he would pray for her every day.

He had. And in his heart, he felt confident that his prayers would bear fruit. The gods would help him protect his love.

But right now, sitting and listening to Aeti, he found his dreams shattered. They had only a day before the draw, and now, with what Aeti had told him, it was certain that he would lose Neri forever.

"I can't imagine my life without her. I love her so much," he said looking at his friend through a film of tears.

Aeti nodded. He knew that Temnet was in love with the girl. Anyone would be. She was sweet and pretty, but highly unfortunate too. Losing both her parents was terrible enough, but gaining a stepmother in the bargain was worse. Her stepmother had played her game impeccably well. The urn was sacrosanct. When the Holy Dwarf would draw Neri's name, everyone would heave a sigh of relief that the deed was done, and they'd all go home and sleep happily, for their daughters were spared, and until next year, the urn that had blighted their lives for a whole month, would once again disappear for a year. Nobody would spare the river bride another thought. They would come to the wedding.

The wedding.

Aeti didn't think of it as a wedding. He believed that it was a sacrifice – a murder disguised as a ritual. When the priests advanced upon the girl, fanning the flames from their lamps into her face, the girl would back up, until she fell backward into the river, screaming not praying. The weights tied to her legs and hands, would sink to the bottom, pulling her along.

It was a wedding that had to happen or the city would erupt in flames. There were many who had arrived here only to watch the wedding. Their arrival meant business for the locals. They and many locals, especially, those whose daughters were past the lottery and safe, were looking forward to the festivities that would accompany the wedding.

But it wasn't Aeti's place to say anything; especially not his place, because he was studying to become a scribe and the temple took care of all his requirements. He had lived his whole life in the temple complex, and after his training as a scribe ended, he was hoping to be picked up by the temple authorities to be a junior priest.

"She's innocent," Temnet lamented, drawing Aeti out of his thoughts.

Aeti nodded again. Neri was as innocent as all those other girls, and she deserved the same chance at life as they did. What was going to happen to her was premeditated murder.

It had to be stopped.

Temnet looked into Aeti's eyes searchingly. "Is there a way out?" he asked.

Aeti scratched his head.

"There's a possibility. Terribly remote and highly improbable, but we might be able to save her by imitating Rahop," he mused.

Temnet looked confused. His mind had suddenly lost its capacity to think.

"By imitating Rahop?" he asked.

Aeti explained.

Temnet listened, nodding every once in a while. When Aeti finished, he had questions.

"But isn't the urn already transferred to the inner-sanctum?"

"It's been," Aeti accepted. Rahop had replaced the clay tablets and taken the urn to the priestess in the morning. The urn was now in the inner sanctum of the temple of *Hapi*, and it could now be accessed only from the priestess's room.

"Even if I could etch and bake the clay tablets with a new name by evening, how are we going to replace them?" Temnet asked, his fingers running over the clay tablet, measuring its thickness and assessing the size of the etching-stick to achieve the right depth and breadth of the marks.

"We can, if the priestess helps," chuckled Aeti.

Temnet looked at his friend. "And you think she will?"

"If we play our game right," Aeti replied.

ᨁᨁ ᨁᨁᨁ ᨁᨁ

It was late afternoon, when the Holy Dwarf found her sitting near the edge of the small pool, watching her reflection in its still water. The priestess was now in her late thirties or early forties. Nobody knew exactly how old or how young she was, and nobody cared, but the Holy Dwarf often wondered about it.

Nobody chose to become a priestess. Some were given to the temple by their parents as their gift to the gods; others were forced to become priestesses by their circumstances, for a priestess bartered her hopes for the assurance of a full belly and a roof upon her head.

Hori-ja too was left upon the steps of the temple complex. She had often wondered about the people who had given her up and why they must have done it. *Was she another mouth to feed in a family already struggling to put two meals together? Or was she a child of a love-priestess who thought that being a priestess of god would be a better calling than becoming a priestess of love? Could she have been left on the hallowed steps because her parents were dead and nobody wanted to care for a child that wasn't theirs?*

She had pondered upon those questions too many times in the past decades. Lately, she had grown tired of the ritual of her endless monolog and stopped questioning her origins. She had come to terms with her reality, which dictated her to remain a virgin all her life, for her body and soul were owned by *Hapi*, the river god.

Hori-ja was now a heavyset woman of middling age, covered in skin that gained a new wrinkle each day. All her life she had lived in the temple complex. Fortunately for the last ten years, she had been the chief priestess of *Hapi*, and so she had her own chambers, but that had been her only luxury – that, and a continuous supply of young priests in her bed. She knew that everyone knew, for the young priests were a babbling lot, but they never talked about it in front of her.

Sometimes she secretly hoped that they would babble. If only the truth came out, and she were divested of her title, she would leave Naqada and go to another city, where, if nothing else, she would become a love-priestess.

Even a love-priestess's life should be more interesting than mine, she thought.

I'm dead. Alive in body, but dead in soul...

As she sat near the pool, looking at her reflection, she saw the ravages of time on her visage. Between her chin and collarbone were sandwiched two rolls of flesh. Her cheeks that once were proud little mounds that would flush pink at the slightest provocation were now listing downward pushed by their loose weight. The corners of her eyes were lined with wrinkles, as was her forehead. Her breasts had turned pendulous and they now competed with *Hapi*'s own.

She noticed the Holy Dwarf's reflection appear by her side, in the pool.

"I have aged," she sighed, without turning to look at him.

"We all have. It is natural to age," replied the dwarf, sitting down beside her, his stunted legs barely touching the surface of the water as he dangled them inside the pool.

"Natural, yes. But women my age have already raised a family. They have children, even grandchildren. They have produced life through their children and felt pride in it. What have I accomplished?"

The dwarf smiled at the reflection of the priestess. The priestess noticed that the dwarf had recently lost two of his front teeth, and that his smile now appeared more hideous than ever. She looked away, but not before the dwarf had caught her expression.

"We are here to accomplish what others can't. We must make it easier for people to carry their burdens by becoming a conduit for their prayers to gods," said the dwarf, ignoring Hori-ja's look of disgust. He had been ignoring the looks she had been giving him, for years.

"Is that enough? What about my own ambitions?" she retorted, then paused and added. "My needs?"

The dwarf's smile deepened into a leer.

"I hear that the young priest who works in the temple of Amun has been working quite hard to satisfy your needs," he coughed.

"Young?" she let out a low whistle. "He was young when he had arrived here, ten years ago. He isn't young anymore. And now that he is a priest himself, he has turned smug. Have you heard of his new ruse? He offers to pray for the young women for nothing. But he doesn't pray for *nothing*, does he?" Hori-ja snickered.

The dwarf knew exactly what she meant. The priest-hood had recently begun to sample earthly delights, the chief among those being the more prurient kind. In past, there had been priests who found the vow of celibacy too hard to keep and like all other men of weaker flesh; they would visit the love-priestesses in disguise. Some had affairs with the priestess-es, but all that was hushed and shushed, and the devotees never learned about it.

Yet, never before they had the temerity to bring women into the temple-complex, nor had they ever stooped into cor-ruption. Offering to pray for a young woman so that she may find a good husband, and in exchange demanding a lustful night with her, was, in his opinion, sinking too low.

The dwarf's eyes returned to his companion's profile. He sat behind her, and that allowed him a view of her thickening neck and back. Her skin was developing the dark spots of age and tiny wrinkles that killed the sparkle of youth were already changing the texture of her skin. She still hadn't turned as obese as some other priests who had given themselves to gluttony, but she had lost the willowy slimness of her youth.

He remembered the day some twenty years ago, when he had first laid eyes upon her. She was willowy thin then, delicate and fresh, a Nile lily in the first bloom of youth. He was young too. A few years older than her but young, and unfortunate, for he was half her height – and while everyone thought of him as a reincarnation of *Bes,* the dwarf god of fertility, and considered him blessed and holy, the young women found him repulsive. He hadn't cared until he had seen Hori-ja.

"You know that there was a time when I loved you," he tendered.

Hori-ja turned to look at him, and asked, "You aren't insinuating that you would like to be sacrificed on the altar of my needs? Are you?"

Why not? The dwarf thought. He was mildly offended. Now, with the first flush of youth gone, Hori-ja appeared a lot more accessible. It wasn't that she was following a vow of chastity, so why couldn't he too leave his copious offerings in the dented vessel that had the dirt of age stuck in its cracks? Had the woman given him the opportunity, she would have realized that his dwarfism didn't affect that part of him, which would interest her the most.

"Of course not. Though I would be delighted to help," he smiled at her.

"Perhaps, in the afterlife, but not in this," she dismissed his overture.

The ugly brute thinks that my charms have faded, thought Hori-ja. *I can still seduce any sixteen-year-old into my bed and bathe him in the fountain of paradise.*

"Think it over, Hori-ja," replied the dwarf. "There are tricks that this old dwarf knows that the young studs don't."

Hori-ja looked at their reflections in the pond and

imagined the dwarf pulling the tricks that he bragged about. The images that flooded in were hilarious, but she didn't laugh.

I've been brought to this by my own follies.

〰 ◊◊◊ 〰

Aeti's anxiety snuck deep into the furrows of his brow. He had made a promise to his friend, and the chances of his fulfilling the promise appeared bleak in the harsh light of the afternoon summer sun.

He stole a glance at them. The priestess sat at the edge of the pond with the Holy Dwarf at her side. Together, they appeared a formidable team. The dwarf was short only in stature. He was a giant in his ability to see afar, so said everyone in the temple-complex.

Aeti swept the steps of the temple of *Hapi* with his eyes on the couple. He had promised to help his friend on a hunch, and now he was worried. All those moments that he thought she was looking at him suggestively, suddenly transformed into figments of his imagination. *They couldn't have been real,* he thought.

She is a lot older than me, he reasoned. *She is a senior priestess, and I am a temporary help, training to be first a scribe and then maybe a priest.*

He watched the odd couple. They were talking with each other, comfortable in a way that could be attributed only to long years of familiarity.

His thoughts made him anxious, making him steal glances at them. His attention wavered, and he suddenly found himself slipping upon the steps. The steps weren't too high, but as he went sailing down ten of them, a cry escaped his lips.

The dwarf and the priestess both turned in time to see him hit the stone-floor with a thud. The priestess was the first to respond, the dwarf pattered behind her, his short feet taking quick steps to keep up with the priestess. When he opened his eyes, Aeti found the priestess's heavy face bent upon his and felt her warm breath upon his neck.

"Are you hurt?" she asked, concern writ large upon her features.

For a moment, he felt so nervous that words escaped him. Then he realized how opportune his situation was. The object of his attention was attending to him. Things like this happened only when the gods willed it to. This was his chance.

"I think I've hurt my back. I hit it on the edge of the last step," he replied, making his voice sound slightly whinny.

The Holy Dwarf too was now crouching next to him.

"Stop whining and get up now, boy," he sent a burst of his hot and pungent breath Aeti's way. "Young boys fall all the time!"

"Don't you see? The child is hurt," The priestess waved the dwarf aside and pushed her palm under Aeti's hip. He winced for her benefit.

"Shhh…" said the priestess. "Now get up slowly. Let your weight fall upon me."

He did as she had asked and pulled himself up with a great display of discomfort. The dwarf watched them intently, as the priestess slid her arm across his shoulder, making his head rest on the side of her bosom.

"Well, well," the dwarf remarked. "I don't see you need my help. Do you, Hori-ja?"

"Not at all," answered Hori-ja giving the dwarf a twisted smile and heaving Aeti up. From the side of his eye, Aeti saw the dwarf's lips curve up in a bitter smile. He looked defeated as he turned and walked away.

Slowly, the priestess and Aeti went around the side of the temple and reached the priestess's chamber behind it.

"Your rooms are on the far side of the complex, aren't

they?" Hori-ja asked him, crushing him to her side, more than she needed to.

"Yes, my lady," he moaned.

"Don't worry. You will stay in my chambers today. Tomorrow, you can go back. Don't say a word about it to your friends or they'll envy you," she whispered in his ear.

"Yes, my lady," he agreed with her. If things happened the way he wanted them to, they would definitely have reasons to be envious of him, for the divine portals didn't open for everyone; but many dreamed of the delights that lay on the other side.

Temnet would arrive after the evening prayers ended. There were many hours between then and now, and Aeti was sure that Hori-ja had some interesting plans for those hours.

Silently, Aeti thanked his gods for helping their plans.

∿∿ 𓏺𓏺𓏺 ∿∿

The Holy Dwarf was indignant.

His anger surged as white and hot as the sun that blazed down upon the stone floor of the temple complex.

Women!

What did they want?

The afternoon heat alone was unbearable. Now combined with the red haze of anger that he felt surging within, it was simply intolerable, even unacceptable.

At this moment, he hated her smugness. He wanted the woman. He had wanted her all these years. She hadn't stopped invading his dreams. In his dreams, he had touched her skin, felt the softness of her thighs, enjoyed the weight of her bosom, and yet, he had never reached the summit, never touched that height of excitement with her, that results in a burst of light that makes everything else invisible for a few moments – when a man and a woman experience that inexplicable pleasure, which makes everything worthwhile.

Even in his dreams, he had never experienced that with her.

And he hadn't, because right before he began his ascent within her, she would look at him and giggle. She would say atrocious things. Even in his dreams she would look above his head and then drop her eyes, and say, "oh, you are down there? I'm sorry, I missed you."

He had loved her once. Perhaps, he would love her always, but at this moment in the harsh light of the sun, he hated her.

All he wanted to do was throw her down on her bed… and…

No, I don't.

Incredibly, even in his anger, he wanted her to consent. He wasn't a devourer of women – he wasn't that kind of scum. He wanted her to come willingly into his arms.

But how could it come to pass?

He had nothing to offer to her. Nothing, except his small deformed self, and a disproportionately big member. If only the gods had been kind and reversed their beneficence, his life would have been so much better!

The afternoon sun burned the skin of his neck and shoulders, as the dwarf walked into the scribal training yard. This was the place where the scribes learned to etch hieroglyphs onto the clay tablets and then bake the tablets for making their etchings permanent. The courtyard was surrounded by different workshops. In afternoons, the workshops would be vacant. No Egyptian who valued his health could be found working in the middle of a summer afternoon. Summer afternoons were for napping. People would throw water upon their reed curtains, darken their rooms, and sleep for two to three hours. He would have done the same, if Hori-ja hadn't snubbed him.

The yard was very hot and uncomfortable, especially

when the furnaces were in use, and right now at least one of them was. This surprised him, for in this heat, the furnaces were usually started early in the morning.

His curiosity made him turn toward the workshop. Someone was inside. The smell of wet clay clung to the smoke that spiraled up through the chimneys, insinuating that someone was baking clay.

Perhaps a scribe, he thought and looked inside.

The hot air in the forge-shop made the whole place look like it was made of molten objects that shape-shifted continuously, their edges turning wavy and their forms morphing and coming alive.

He was right. The young man who sat hunched working the bellows was studying to be a scribe. He knew him by sight, but not by name. The Holy Dwarf entered the workshop and approached the young man. The infernal sound made by the furnace drowned the clacking of his reed-sandals. The young man hadn't heard him and he was still focused on raising the heat of the furnace, when the dwarf reached behind him and took a peek at a few deformed clay tablets that he had kept aside.

They were the same shape and size as the ones used in the river bride's urn. He squinted his eyes to get a better look at the hieroglyphs.

"Mutret?" he enunciated the name.

The young man sprang to his feet, letting the bellows clatter to the ground, shock and fear writ large upon his features.

"Your holiness," he stuttered, as he bowed low and curtsied.

"What's your name?" asked the Holy Dwarf.

"Temnet," he answered, his voice still trembling.

"Ah…yes, I thought I recognized you," said the dwarf, his eyes scanning Temnet's face. "Tell me, Temnet," he asked. "Why is it that you are here melting your skin at this hour of Ra?"

"I had some clay tablets to bake," he replied.

"Three hundred and nineteen, I suppose," chuckled the dwarf.

Temnet stared at the dwarf in shock. *How could he know?*

"And now you are wondering, how I learned about it? Aren't you?" the dwarf asked, waving him to sit down. "You better sit down or I'll cramp my neck, talking to you."

"Yes, your holiness," Temnet replied and hurriedly sat down.

Then he told the dwarf everything, and how he and his friend Aeti had planned to swap Neri's name with Mutret's.

"Mutret deserves it," he said, ending his story.

"I don't doubt it for a moment," the Holy Dwarf replied. "But what you have done is wrong, and I've caught you red-handed. You can lose your hand for this."

"Yes, I know but…" said Temnet, wondering why he felt that the dwarf had more to say on the matter."

"Shhh…," said the dwarf, raising his thick blocky hand and placing it upon his shoulder. "I will not report you," his said, "but there is something you must do."

Temnet's visitor left after an hour.

〰〰 ◊◊◊ 〰〰

After the tablets were baked, Temnet had waited for the furnace to cool down. He had then taken the tablets to his room and brushed the ash off them. They were now as clean as the tablets that he would be replacing.

Temnet found it surprising that he wasn't terrified at the idea of burgling a temple. He didn't fear the wrath of the gods, not even of *Hapi*, who he trusted would be hopping mad upon discovering the swap. He perceived the whole thing as his and

Aeti's attempt to right a wrong.

He and Aeti had a plan in place, and while the plan required that they matched their moves with apparently impossible precision, he was confident that they would be able to pull it off, especially now, when the Holy Dwarf had himself blessed their plan to save Neri.

He felt it. *No, he knew it.* Neri will not die and *Hapi* will find his bride.

The darkness of the night was Temnet's friend in disguise. In a piece of cloth, he had packed the clay tablets tight, and used a piece of linen to tie the packet to his chest. Aeti had cleaned the priestess's rooms in the past, and he had explained the layout of the place to Temnet. The only way to get inside the priestess's living chambers was through the window in the antechamber, and other than the main door of the temple, the only way of reaching the inner-sanctum was through the priestess's own bedchamber.

Unfortunately, he had not been able to meet Aeti that evening and so he was completely clueless about how the plan had progressed at Aeti's end. If things had gone as planned, then right now Aeti would be in the priestess's bed, entertaining her and waiting for Temnet to arrive and do his part. If Aeti had failed to keep his part in the bargain, Temnet would be running the risk of being caught, for the priests and the priestesses were light sleepers. They had trained their bodies to wake up before dawn.

What if Aeti was wrong about the priestess? Temnet thought anxiously, as he found the open window on the side of the priestess's dwelling. He hoisted himself upon the sill of the window and dropped inside, crouching as he went down so that he landed as noiselessly as he could.

The first sound he heard inside were giggles. Then he heard Aeti's voice.

"My lady, you are divine," he was saying. If Temnet

weren't so tensed, he would have had to suppress his laughter.

"Don't call me that," the hoarse voice of Hori-ja complained. "At least not when you are in bed with me. Call me Hori," she said, her voice muffled, sandwiched between the sounds of wet kisses.

"Hori," said Aeti, "lie still. Let me serve your body with my lips."

Temnet stood behind the wall that separated the antechamber from the bedchamber. The antechamber was a simple room with a low table and few low stools. It was perhaps the room where she met other priests and priestesses. A reed curtain hung from the top edge of the door that separated the two chambers. Temnet inched closer and moved the curtain slightly aside.

The priestess's bedchamber was smaller than Temnet's own chamber at home. Her bed stood against the far wall near the window, a lamp burned in a sconce embedded in the wall.

"Lay your head here," said Aeti, picking up the feather pillow and placing it at the feet of the bed, toward the door behind which Temnet stood.

"Why?" asked Hori-ja. She wasn't used to receiving instructions.

"So that when the moon casts its silver light upon your sweet body, my mouth is guided right," Aeti replied. He had rehearsed it.

Even in his precarious situation, Temnet couldn't help admiring his friend's gumption and charisma.

He watched as Hori-ja picked up her substantial mass and pivoted upon her hips to place her head on the pillow. Aeti knelt beside her, touching and fondling her breasts before parting her legs slightly. Then he bent his head down upon the peaks of her breasts, first teasing one then the other, making Hori-ja's body spasm with a desire that was quickly beginning to heighten.

For a moment, Temnet wanted to stand there and watch the scene unfold. He wasn't as experienced as Aeti was. The image of a voluptuous middling woman being pleasured by a young man would remain etched in his mind for a very long time.

He tried to imagine himself in place of Aeti. As the hand of the woman reached her own seat of pleasure, the scene dissolved into Neri's sweet face, her beautiful green eyes filled with trust.

If I don't move now, Neri would be dead. He chided himself for not being able to control his voyeuristic curiosity. And then there was Aeti, who had risked his life for Temnet's happiness, and was now making the priestess mewl and moan with his maneuvers.

So Temnet tried to ignore the distracting sounds of sucking and licking, and moaning and groaning, and he slowly sank to his knees and crawled inside the room. On fours, he moved noiselessly toward the door that he knew would take him into the inner sanctum, the bag of tablets secure against his chest.

Once inside, Temnet worked with such alacrity and precision that he surprised even himself.

Outside, the tempo was building. When Temnet crawled back into the priestess's bedchamber, he saw that Aeti was already past the divine portals, and into the priestess's personal shrine. The moonlit bed with its crumpled sheet, looked like the surface of Nile broken by the cataracts, and the couple upon it trying to conquer the rush of their passion, seemed like a galley in the river, pitching and rolling, swaying and surging.

The priestess's eyes were closed and so were Aeti's, for inside the shrine of the goddess that shook beneath him with pleasure, he was about to make his final offering.

The crescendo was building as Temnet crawled out of the bedchamber and stood up straight.

"Oh, Aeti! Aeti! Aeti!" the priestess called out.

ᗺᗺ ◊◊◊ ᗺᗺ

The draw happened a week later.

Three hundred and nineteen girls awaited the pronouncement. They had spent a whole month preparing to become the bride of *Hapi*. Each of them had been trained to accept that if her name came up, she should feel fortunate. They knew that the bride's last night would be celebrated. The bride would sit on one side of a pair of scales, and the parents of the girls who weren't selected would add pitchers of *heqt*, clothes, and food to the other side, until the scales balanced. The things would then be given away to the poor. So the poor would rejoice, same as the parents whose daughters were spared.

The girls and their parents were not the only ones who had gathered for the draw, but they were the only ones who did not look happy. Their lips were twisted to control the tears that sat in the corners of their eyes, ready to roll down any moment.

For most others, it was a time of celebration. The tourists, the officials, the musicians, the dancers, and the vendors… nearly half the population of Naqada was there, waiting for the festivities that would begin shortly after the Holy Dwarf announced the name of the bride. Everyone waited patiently – even though the sun got hotter and the sand followed suit. They cooled themselves the best they could, fanning themselves with papyrus fans and drinking coconut water. Some were even sprinkling water upon their bodies.

Among the girls, who were still praying silently, was Neri. She hadn't slept the night before, and for some odd reason that she couldn't place her finger upon, she had a premonition that her name would be called out. Next to her, holding Neri's hand in a vice-grip stood her stepmother, Mutret.

She had draped herself in her finest dress for the occasion. After all, Mutret was sure that she would be the one walking the river-bride to the scales.

Just ten steps above the stone floor where the girls and their families stood, right at the entrance of the temple of *Hapi,* stood a table upon which the urn was placed.

The girls and their parents knew that urn by sight. It had tortured their imagination for a whole month. They knew that somewhere in its belly, the urn carried the weapon that could destroy their happiness – the weapon was in shape of a clay tablet, with a name on it. They looked at the urn with such apprehension that their whole existence centered upon the secret inside it. It had tormented them for so long, that they were now hypnotized by it, oblivious to the two figures that stood behind the urn.

First, there was the tall one. A portly, rather majestic looking woman, who wore a white tunic that was fastened under her sumptuous, near-pendulous breasts and whose hair was made into a coiffure, decorated with flowers and bells. She also wore garlands and armlets of white lilies. She was the priestess of *Hapi*, his perpetual bride – the forever virgin.

And then there was the short one. He was the Holy Dwarf. The dwarf wore a *shenti* under a rotund belly that made the urn look imperfect. He stood upon a stool but he was still about a full hand shorter than the priestess. His stubby fingers were drumming the table, giving away his impatience to get the task done.

The dwarf's task was to pick the name of *Hapi*'s bride.

The young man, who stood behind the priestess, put the trumpet to his lips and blew hard, his nostrils flaring and his cheeks puffing up. The sound of the trumpet carried above the heads of the audience, ricocheting and echoing, it filled the place and marked the beginning of the ceremony.

Temnet caught the eyes of Aeti, the trumpet-blower, and smiled. Aeti looked happy and content this morning – and unlike his earlier self, he beamed with confidence.

The ceremony began with the burning of incense and singing of the hymns to *Hapi*. Then the jar of Nile water was brought to the steps. The jar would be broken right over the head of the girl who would be chosen to become the river bride.

The face of the Holy Dwarf remained as inscrutable as ever, as he prepared himself to do a duty that he didn't relish. His expressions seldom gave his feelings away, and so he was the only one who realized how heavy his heart felt as he dipped the ladle into the urn and stirred the tablets within. Seven times he would churn it clockwise so that the rising sun may bless it. Then seven times he would churn it counterclockwise so that the setting sun may bless it.

"Give us her name," a chant went up from the crowd. Others picked it up quickly.

"Give us the name of the bride," the crowd roiled and cried.

Of the three hundred and nineteen girls, a few fainted. Others stood still, their faces as expressionless as the dwarf's, ready to accept their fate and save their city.

The Holy Dwarf set the ladle aside, and dipped his hand into the urn. The chants stopped as everyone waited with baited breath, watching the dwarf's hand come out again – with a tablet held in his thick misshapen hand.

He turned the tablet to read the inscription on it, but stopped before he could articulate the name on it.

"Give us the name," the chants began again.

The Holy Dwarf swallowed.

He turned to look at the priestess. Under the layers of fat, beneath the skin that was beginning to wilt, he saw the fourteen-year-old girl who had stolen his heart.

"Give us the name of the bride," the chants grew louder.

"Give them the name," the priestess prodded.

The dwarf swallowed again. Even though he was at the helm of it, even though he had been confident that everything would work out fine, he found his anxiety rising.

What if something went wrong?

He knew that she didn't love him back. She would sleep with every runt in the temple complex, but she wouldn't let him hide his ugly face in her bosom. She hated him, for he was born with the element of divinity. She rejected him because he was born in the form of *Bes* – the god of love and fertility.

And yet, he wanted her to be safe. She had been safe, but he had meddled and made her unsafe. All because he had been angry, and because the need for vengeance had filled his heart and soul, and turned him blind to the risks.

Once the name passed his lips, there would be no going back.

"Give them the name," Hori-ja exhorted him again. The crowd would become unruly if he didn't offer them the name quickly. They had been waiting for this moment for days, even weeks.

He made up his mind. He gathered his courage and placed his trust in the gullibility of the common folk. If he didn't lose his nerve, everything would slip back into place.

He coughed to clear his throat, and then held up his hand.

"Hori-ja," he said, his voice carrying across the courtyard, loud, clear, and confident.

"What?" whispered Hori-ja. Her face losing its color and turning pasty white, she turned and looked at the Holy Dwarf with her wide, fearful eyes.

The crowd went silent.

"What was it, again?" someone shouted.

Anger roiled inside Hori-ja. It was clear to her that the dwarf was exacting his revenge.

"This is impossible," she hissed as she snatched away

the tablet from the dwarf's hand.

"Hori-ja," the dwarf entreated, but the priestess held out her hand. The crowd was getting restless, so the dwarf waved to them and asked them to settle down.

"Aeti," Hori-ja turned to her newest paramour who stood behind them and thrust the tablet in his hand. Then she whispered loudly, her voice grating and urgent. "Read the tablet. What is the name on it?"

Aeti dutifully took the tablet and in a low voice meant only for her, he read out her name.

Hori-ja shook with anger.

She would throttle that miserable excuse of a man; she would bundle him up into a papyrus mat and throw him into the Nile…

The dwarf watched her. He knew exactly what she was thinking, and he knew that his moment was either now or never.

He brought his hand to his face, ostensibly to scratch his nose, and hiding his mouth from the crowd, he addressed her.

"Hori-ja, trust me. I'll let no harm come to you, I promise."

She heard him but more than his words, she heard the conviction and the promise in his voice. For an inexplicable reason, her name was in the urn, and it had been drawn in front of the populace of Thinis. It would be impossible for her to escape her fate, unless the gods intervened.

And the Holy Dwarf was thought to be the incarnation of god Bes.

She could do nothing but pray…and plan her escape. *Tonight, she would pack her things and escape to Saqqara.*

"Hori-ja," The dwarf called out, his voice stronger this time. "The name is Hori-ja. *Hapi* wants his bride to come home," he added.

Murmurs went up in the crowd. People were mesmerized. It was unprecedented but divine, for the gods had their own mysterious ways of doing things. Some of the murmurs reached the Holy Dwarf's ears.

"*Hapi* wants a virgin bride. Who could then be better than the priestess herself?" someone in the crowd cried.

The Holy Dwarf took his cue and raised his voice once again.

"*Hapi* wants to choose his own bride this year and if he doesn't claim his own by tomorrow morning, we shall send Hori-ja to him as his bride."

In the crowd, Neri nearly fainted with relief. When she got hold of herself, she turned around and found her stepmother gone.

Temnet had seen Mutret leave in a huff, He also saw Rahop sneak away in a different direction, possibly to avoid Mutret.

He found his way to Neri, who caught his eyes and smiled, tears rolling down her cheeks.

Temnet still had work to do, but this was their moment.

꩜ ꩜

The next morning, the body of a woman washed up on the bank of Nile. The fishermen were always the first to arrive on the riverbank, so nobody was surprised that they were the ones who found the body. Around her neck, the woman wore an amulet, a small clay tablet with hieroglyphs.

"*Hapi* has chosen his bride," they shouted as they carried the body into the temple complex.

The Holy Dwarf had just finished his ablutions.

"*Hapi* has selected his bride," the fisherman who had led them to the temple, said to the Holy Dwarf.

"Not young, is she?" asked the dwarf.

"No," they replied.

"Nor a virgin?" asked the dwarf again.

They giggled.

"How can we know that?" asked one of them, his tongue darting back and forth through his broken yellow teeth.

"If you knew who she was, you would know that she isn't a virgin," said the dwarf.

"I know," said Temnet stepping out of the crowd. He had been there the previous night. *When Hapi had claimed the woman as his own.*

"Do you know her?" asked the Holy Dwarf.

"Yes, I do. She lived in the house next to mine. She is Mutret, the widow of Meriptah the trader, and she isn't a virgin."

"There's a tablet with an inscription around her neck," said Temnet, pointing to the baked tablet that hung as a pendant on a black thread that went around the corpse's neck.

"A message from Hapi," a murmur went up in the crowd. It was quickly taken up by the others and turned into a chant.

"Bring it to me," commanded the dwarf.

The men quickly removed the tablet and handed it over to the Holy Dwarf.

The dwarf took the clay tablet, squinted his eyes, and read aloud.

"I, Hapi, have chosen my bride for this year and for the years to come. Don't send me another, for they squabble among themselves and make me miserable. I take this woman as my last human bride in the hope that she will control the others," recited the dwarf.

"She was the last bride that *Hapi* would ever take," the dwarf concluded.

Then he stopped and looked at the crowd.

Behind the dwarf sat the Priestess of Hapi with her eyes closed. She slowly opened her eyes and addressed the crowd.

"He didn't want me to go live with him and leave all of you, my only children alone. He came into my dreams and told me this, when I entreated him to take me away," intoned the Priestess. She moved her eyes over every face in the group, and talked to each of them, mesmerizing them with her eyes.

Heads began to nod.

The dream of a priest or a priestess was a communication received directly from the gods. The people of Naqada had their own businesses to tend to, and when the priestess and the Holy Dwarf spoke in one voice, they nodded their heads and the courtyard began to buzz with their remarks.

"The gods work through us," said one.

"And they speak to us through the priests," philosophized another.

"So Hapi doesn't want another bride? He must have thousands now," mused aloud a third.

"A thousand wives? My one wife drives me mad," laughed a fourth.

The Holy Dwarf's voice rose to drown theirs.

"The ceremony shall be held this afternoon and the temple will donate the grains and *heqt* equal to the bride's weight to the poor and needy. Hapi's last bride will be sent to him in full glory," he said.

Everyone cheered, and then they went away to spread the news.

ᴡᴡ ууу ᴡᴡ

After the sun had set and darkness had fallen, the priestess opened the door of her chambers to admit her oldest and most ardent admirer in. He had kept his promise. He had let no harm come to her. She had no inkling of what had transpired, but the dwarf had saved her from certain death.

He was indeed divine.

The dwarf looked up and saw her face. It was clear that the sun had risen in his life once again.

She looked down upon his countenance. His broad nose, his rheumy eyes, his mouth filled with broken and misshapen teeth – they didn't look all that repugnant today. Neither his oddly shaped feet that looked awkward in his papyrus sandals, nor his globular belly repelled her today. And, if truth were told, she had often wondered what kind of monster lay under his *shenti*. Today, she would find out. But more than anything else, she felt that she owed him her love and gratitude.

He had saved her life, and no payment was big enough for her savior.

"Come in," she said, her voice sweet as honey.

He stepped in and took in the interiors of her living chamber. Then he followed her inside her bedchamber, which had been the focal point of his tortured existence all these years. The room was sparsely furnished, but her bed was luxurious. She got into the bed first and spread her arms to welcome him. As he climbed the bed, somewhat laboriously, for it was high, she moved her hand to unclip her tunic.

"Don't," said the dwarf, as he pushed her down and his stubby fingers found the clip that held her tunic together.

It was a moment that he had dreamed about for years, and he was going to do it all, his way.

Many hours later, when he hopped off the bed and picked up his *shenti* from the floor where it had landed last night, he heard Hori-ja's voice.

"I'll wait for you tonight," she said, her voice lusciously husky.

The dwarf smiled inwardly.
He had found himself a kindred soul.

Historical Notes:

Historians are divided on whether the ritual of sacrificing a virgin to appease Nile is a myth or a fact.

In 1878, Professor G. Ebers wrote a book called, "Picturesque Egypt Volume I," in which he included an image of a woman wearing little except a translucent veil, standing on a stone platform, about to be tossed into the river. The corresponding text mentions that a statue is, "to this day" tossed into Nile "as a substitute of the fair virgin."

The tradition of live sacrifice had in all probability died before the Old Kingdom, because there are no historical records of the practice.

Story Two

THE NECROPHILE'S RING

~ | New Kingdom | ~

THE NECROPHILE'S RING

Ten days had passed since the Burning took place but its fire still smoldered in Ita's heart. Her carefree innocence had been consumed by a scorching combination of guilt and suspicion.

She was inside the embalming chamber, tidying up the chest of drawers that contained the mummification tools. The light that entered through its wide windows was turning a bright shade of rust as the sun was setting upon the city of Thinis that sprawled upon the banks of Nile.

The shiny bronze knobs of the top five drawers in the chest that stood against the wall, testified to the drawers being in regular use. She went through them, one by one, cleaning the tools and organizing them.

The patina-encrusted knob of the sixth and the lowest drawer, which was seldom used, made her stop. This drawer, she knew, was filled with tools left unused for many years. Inside, she expected to find them sheathed in black and green, same as the knob outside. Who knew what horrors were hidden within?

Possibly a lizard's nest or even a colony of white ants, she thought.

Ita looked at the last drawer once again. She would bring along a few lemons tomorrow, and the bronze of the knob would shine so bright that it would put the other five knobs to shame.

But she didn't want to leave the last drawer unattended. The feeling of not completing what she started, of leaving things unfinished, had become the bane of her life. It had stolen her sleep by replacing her sweet dreams with nightmares that kept her awake half the night.

She was going to tidy up that last drawer. If she finished cleaning it, she might sleep better.

Ita sat down upon the floor and pulled the drawer out. The drawer resisted slightly, but then gave way and slid out. She had expected it to resist more for nobody had opened it in years, and yet she was happy that she didn't have to struggle with it.

One look inside allayed her fears. There was no lizard inside, angrily staring at her for disturbing her nest, and there weren't any ants, white or otherwise, scurrying about busily. Only the tools were there – old and crusted, waiting to be sent away to the blacksmiths so that they could be melted and formed anew.

She gingerly lifted the brain-scooper, the one with a little hook at the top. It was special. Her father had told her that it was more than a hundred years old and it had belonged to her great-grandfather. She wondered if her father was clinging on to these old tools for emotional reasons. She removed them, one by one.

The different obsidian knives that were used to make clean deep cuts at the sides of the dead for removing their entrails; the hooks to keep the skin of the cadavers tightened during evisceration; the sewing needles that had turned blind from crusting - everything inside was old. As she picked the obsidian blades out carefully, a ray of the setting sun fell into the open drawer and made something gleam and sparkle.

She placed the blade down on the floor, and picked up the shiny little piece of metal, recognizing it immediately.

It was the ring – a simple gold ring, with the hieroglyphs of a name. It wasn't the ring of *shen,* the kind people wore to ward off bad luck. It had no deity, no stone to bring luck or thwart the evil spirits. It just had a name on it. Looking up and through the window, she saw the sky slowly change its color to a deep, dark gray.

The ring had no reason to be there. Not inside that drawer, which could be opened only intentionally and deliberately, and never by mistake.

It could mean only one thing.

She felt the souls of the dead closing in upon hers, jostling with one another and pointing fingers at her.

"You left your work unfinished," screeched the souls that were gathering around her, their voices grating and rasping.

Ita vomited upon the tools that she had removed from the drawer. Then she sat there listless and silent, holding the ring in her hand. After a very long time, when the sky outside had turned as dark and melancholy as her soul, she picked up the obsidian knife and placed it inside her leather pouch.

She was going to end this story.

᠊᠊᠊ ⵣⵣⵣ ᠊᠊᠊

The city center was a busy and important place. Those deemed worthy of a spectacular punishment, were brought here so that they were either executed or divested of one of their body parts, in front of everyone who wanted to watch. The place where the executions were carried out was right in the center, where the five city roads converged. It was a square platform, set about ten cubits high and forty cubits on all its four sides. Unlike the temples and the palaces, this platform was made completely of roughly hewn granite. This was the place where disfigurements were meted out to punish the erring every week, and every few months a convict who had been found guilty of being disloyal to Pharaoh was made to consume poison. Once a year, those convicted of high treason, were impaled for their transgressions against the divine ruler of Egypt.

Those deaths were normal. When they were scheduled, the drummers would go around the city announcing the impending execution; and the locals, mostly the unemployed, the beggars, and the street urchins, would gather to witness a man or a woman sit upon a stake, and then go back to doing nothing.

No special preparations were done for those regular executions. They would just bring out their old wooden equipment, check if the stake's tip was sharp enough, and they would be ready.

But today was different.

Today, they were bringing in vats of pig-fat and dried reeds and wood. A cage was set up in the middle of the execution square, within which they were beginning to spread the reeds. In the city of Thinis, news travelled faster than a galley upon the Nile, for it rode upon the tongues of the street urchins. Before noon, almost everyone in the city had learned that in two days, there shall be a new kind of execution.

The vats of fat and the dried reeds indicated that there would be an execution of the kind that neither the city nor Egypt had witnessed in the last hundred years.

Rumors were rife that a man would be burned alive, for a transgression so evil that it defied both morality and logic. The man, said the city-murmurs, was young, not more than twenty and good-looking too. All these factors further enhanced the morbid curiosity of the citizens of Thinis, and sent them to the city center in droves.

Thinis was a hoary old city, even older than the pyramids. It was the capital of Upper Egypt before the time of the pyramid-building kings, but more than a thousand years had passed since, and now it was little more than a sleepy city with cracked walls and dusty roads.

The people of Thinis exhibited a character similar to that of their city. They were generally a bored lot, and something as exciting as a man being burned alive, made them throng to the city center. Those from nearby towns had already begun to arrive. Some had brought along reed mats so that they could keep their place. Others who lived nearby had the perspicacity to see a business opportunity and so they had brought every child aged between two and twelve from their neighborhood and promised to buy them sweetmeats if they vacated their seats for the last-minute arrivals. The last-minute arrivals would pay well for getting a front seat.

The small vendors too had begun to arrive. The sellers of reed mats were the first ones. Later in the day and toward the evening, others would follow. The juice-sellers, the snack-sellers, even a few offering to fill the water-skins of the all-nighters for a consideration.

The city center hadn't seen such activity for a very long time. One of the travelers from the north had mentioned that it reminded him of the crowd that Pharaoh Amenemhat Nubkaure's *Heb-set* festival had attracted two years ago. The first *Heb-set* of a Pharaoh was celebrated only when he had ruled for thirty years. It wasn't an event that happened very often, and so all Egyptians, the suckling babes to the rheumy-eyed doddering old men and women, attended it.

This too was such an event.

Ita stood like a statue in the bustling crowd. As people milled around her to get a better view of the pyre, she stood like she were made of stone.

Perhaps, I am. I am made of stone, she thought.

᙭᙭ ᑫᑫᑫ ᙭᙭

The villa of the nome-treasurer Senitef that sprawled upon the western bank of Nile was located on the outer rim of Thinis. Thinis was so old that the ruins of the past constructions still stood amidst the new buildings. Some were almost ancient, and had begun to look like scars that added an element of interest to the face of Thinis, while others that were more recent were akin to sores and wounds that the eyes hoped to avoid.

Senitef's father had been one of the most respected men in all of Thinis, and was considered second only to the Governor. A year ago, he had died and Senitef had taken over his father's position at the office of the Governor.

Ita was on her way to Senitef's villa. She worked there, just as her mother did, and every day until now she had smiled, danced, and pirouetted whenever she walked this path of beaten dirt that meandered through the farms and had palms growing on either side.

Today, however, her face was streaked with tears and her steps were heavy with the burden of sorrow. The knowledge that she would not meet anyone on her way to the villa nibbled away the mask of indifference that she had been wearing since the tribunal had given its verdict, and the Governor, in his role of the Priest of *Ma'at,* had passed the sentence.

Tears forced their way out of her eyes, wetting her face, making her feel the sting of the breeze. Her memories jostled with one another, shouting at her to look at them, while with each step she took, she tried to slam the door back, trying to keep them inside. But she failed each time she tried. Through the crack of the door in her mind, her insistent memories tumbled out one by one, and rushed to occupy her thoughts.

"Drive me insane," she grumbled at the memories as she stubbed her toe on a rock that jutted out of the ground. "Be quick, and make me mad. For then I won't feel the pain and the tears will stop. At least then I'll be able to see where I am going!"

In distance, on the horizon, she could see the white walls of the yard of the villa. The boundary wall was characteristic of the houses of the rich. A random thought struggled through the tragic ones jostling for her attention and reached her.

What happened within those walls? What kind of lives they lived after dark? What thoughts made them happy, or tortured them?

Ita worked there. She was a scullery maid who was recently promoted to cleaning the living-chambers of the master and his wife. An embalmer's daughter, she had grown up surrounded by the dead as much as the living.

When she was a little girl, she would patter in and out of the embalming chamber that her father owned.

The embalming chambers were simple rectangular buildings, each housing three to four inclined platforms less than two cubits high, with a palm-length high parapet wall that ran around each. The bodies rested on these platforms when they were being prepared for their journey onward. The floors were paved with stones that had begun to turn smooth after having been used for centuries. She had never felt dread or revulsion in there – for the dead were brought in so that they could be prepared for their afterlife, and the embalmers were there only to ensure that when the *ka* of the dead came looking for its body, it was found intact.

When she had turned thirteen, her mother had decided that Ita needed to become responsible for herself, and so she had taken Ita along to Lord Senitef's villa where she worked as a cook. Six years had passed since. Now nineteen, she should have been married and a mother herself, but she was quite content with the life she had been leading, and in love too.

But that ended yesterday. It ended with the verdict.

Ita wiped away her tears again.

Until yesterday afternoon she had been in love, but now she wasn't sure. For one whole week, she had tried to keep her trust in him unbroken, despite everything; but when *Ma'at*, the goddess of justice, had spoken through her priest, Ita's trust had wavered.

She had been there, when the Governor who wore the crown and the pectoral of the Priest of *Ma'at,* had announced that the tribunal, which comprised three most important men of Thinis, had found her Aneni guilty of the unspeakable crime. She had gone there alone – secretly, without telling anyone. She hadn't even told her parents, for if they knew, they would dig a well in their own backyard and throw her in it. After the city guards had taken Aneni away, her parents had told Ita that they wanted her to forget him.

The crime they said he had committed was a taboo imposed by the gods. He had destroyed the honor of the embalming chamber, where the living left their dead relatives, trusting the embalmers to protect the honor of their loved ones as their bodies were prepared for their journey into the afterlife.

For Ita, the embalming chamber was more than just a room where dead bodies were prepared. For her, it was where her father worked. The embalming chamber was full of her childhood memories, and yet, it had suddenly begun to terrorize her.

That Aneni, her beautiful, young, caring lover could do something so odious, was difficult for her to accept. The heinousness of his crime was now being talked about not only in Thinis, but she was sure, in the whole Egypt.

Her Aneni couldn't be that wretched man.

But he was not just indicted; he was convicted.

"I'm not sure," she murmured to herself. "I don't know

whom to trust."

The villa on the horizon now appeared nearer and bigger. This meant that she had been walking - crying and walking.

The crying had to stop.

She couldn't kill herself over what Aneni did.

What he did was beyond terrible, and a woman who shed tears upon such a man should herself be doomed to forever search for her own body in the afterlife. His punishment was just and right. They would burn him alive. Nobody alive had ever seen anyone executed by burning, but she had heard that they made sure that only the ashes remained. No body, no burial, and no possibility of an afterlife.

He will be gone from the world forever!

The tears came again.

She sniffled and tried to hold them back but failed. A week ago, the day of that evil deed, she had walked the same way. That day, her heart had wings and it fluttered ahead of her, beckoning her to follow it, for Aneni too worked at Lord Senitef's villa, and going to work meant going to him.

But that was then.

When their work was done, she had gone into the granary with Aneni. He was Lord Senitef's scribe and the manager of the granary, and so he had the keys. That day they had…

She stopped.

This has to stop, she told herself, but her heart revolted. Ita sank to her knees and covered her face with her palms, trying to keep herself together. After many long moments, slowly she removed her palms and looked ahead. The villa was now very close. All she had to do was reach there. The memories, the fears, the thoughts, would all disappear. Lord Senitef's villa was a magnificent place full of sounds and smells and colors, which would drown her senses and numb the pain that kept searing through her heart, incessantly.

She stood up again and broke into a run. When she reached the villa, she was out of breath, and when she entered, a few drops of sweat were already glistening upon her forehead.

The first voice that reached her was her Mistress's.

"Ita, you are late again," she called from the breakfast table, where she sat with her daughters.

Her Mistress's accusation was the sweetest voice that she had heard since morning. It reached inside her head and strangulated the tortuous thoughts that she had been having since morning.

"I apologize, Lady Senitef. I'll get to work immediately," she replied as a smile broke across her face.

"Clean my husband's bedchamber first, then you can do mine," Lady Senitef who was attempting to feed her younger daughter of three, shot her a perfunctory glance.

Ita's heart sank.

The deluge of her recent sorrow had unanchored her other concerns and shoved them into oblivion. Now the biggest of them all, came charging upon her like a fire-spitting monster.

"Lady Senitef," she asked, her voice quavering. "Has Lord Senitef left?"

Her question reaped no answer. Lady Senitef's three-year-old daughter had secured her attention by coughing her porridge out upon her mother's lovely aquamarine gown.

Ita's instinct told her that if she lingered about, Lady Senitef's anger would be vented upon her, and so to disappear from the scene, she hastened to the entrance that led into Senitef's bedchamber.

She cracked the door open, slipped behind the curtains and parted them gingerly.

Inside, Lady Senitef's husband stood stark naked, his eyes staring right into Ita's.

᭦᭦᭦ ᛃ᛭᛭ ᭦᭦᭦

This was the yard of the condemned. A tall stonewall, the height of six men, surrounded it. The stonewall was mostly to keep people out rather than to stop the convicts from escaping, for the wells of the living dead that dotted the yard were impossible to leave. The wells were deep shafts, again as deep as the surrounding stonewall was high. Inside these wells, a man could sit or at most lie with his knees bent.

Aneni was in one of these wells. It was a deep hole with smooth and sheer walls that rose up straight, converging into a disk of light. The well was dug not to provide life but to contain it. Outside, on the ground, a parapet wall that came up to the knee of a grown man rose around the well. Each day, morning and evening, guards came to lower food and water to the men and women who were arraigned inside these prison wells, but when they came to his well, they spit upon him. Sometimes they threw him a few crumbs, but mostly they just abused him and walked past.

Lover of the Dead!
Turd of Seth!
The Godless Grunge!
Blasphemer!

The insults hurt him in the beginning, but then hunger and thirst began to hurt him more, and the insults turned into noise. At times, he had even found himself waiting to hear the insults, because sometimes, they would throw in a water skin with a few drops clinging to its insides, or a rotten piece of *dhurra* bread. He would scramble to catch whatever they threw in, to prevent it from falling upon the floor that was covered with excreta. Layers after layers of it, had caked upon the floor, and now his own too. He couldn't imagine how it would be to eat something off the floor.

His responses were slowing down but his senses had become heightened, especially his sense of sound, because all his other senses, of sight, touch, taste, even smell, had nothing new to sample. He had memorized the cracks and the shapes of the stones that were used to line the wall and had begun to see shapes in them, and he had also become used to the smells of ordure and sweat... and the taste of his own tears.

He was lowered in this well a week ago, for a crime so heinous that when his sentence was read out, the Governor in his role as the Priest of *Ma'at* had asked the details of it to be stricken out from the records.

Aneni was a good-looking young man, with a regular life. He worked as a granary manager for one of the richest men in the city, and he was in love too. Everything had been wonderful until a week ago. Now he was a prisoner who sat in this well of the living dead, covered in filth, his hair matted with sweat, urine, and feces.

The young handsome man had disappeared without a trace.

"How can I prove anything? I'm stuck here," he had asked the magistrate who had arrived yesterday and peeked into the well, covering his nose with a piece of silk. A fragrant beeswax cone placed upon his head was melting to keep him cool. Aneni knew because a few drops had splashed upon him.

"It appears difficult, doesn't it?" he had laughed through his broken teeth.

Then he had read his execution order to Aneni, his voice muffled by the silk he had wrapped around his nose.

"Aneni, the defiler of the dead, shall be put to death by burning. This shall be his punishment for dishonoring the dead body of Banet, the daughter of Remram and wife of Kherit. This execution order was signed and stamped by the Governor as the Priest of *Ma'at*. Unless a proof of his innocence is furnished to the Governor, before the third hour of *Ra* on the day after tomorrow, the accused Aneni will be executed at the execution square in the city center. The tribunal has decided that death by burning is the only adequate and appropriate punishment in this case, as one who perpetrates such heinous crimes in this world, must not be allowed into the afterlife."

The magistrate had left quickly, like he didn't want to spend another moment in the company of someone who had been banished not just from this life, but also from the afterlife.

Aneni broke down and prayed to all the deities he knew of. He even prayed to *Anubis,* for he was the patron god of Ita's family. As he prayed inside the well, outside, the sky darkened.

Soon he would be leaving the land of the living. Aneni hadn't seen a man burned to death, but he had witnessed a few executions by impalement, and so he could imagine the crowd going wild outside the walls of the prison. There would be drunken brawls among those who would have come from the nearby towns and villages to witness justice being served. Street-wenches and love-priestesses would be selling their wares to the travelers and the thrill-seekers of the city alike – for them, business would be brisk and quick. And the cream of the whole experience would be the gossip. They would lap up every rumor, every detail – real or imaginary.

Aneni tore his thoughts away and tried to concentrate on the face of Ita. Oddly, her face kept breaking into small wispy pieces that floated away from him. After many failed attempts, only for a few moments, he was able to keep Ita's face anchored in front of his closed eyes. He quickly said what was important, and hoped that the gods and goddesses that dwelled in both their hearts would convey his message to her.

A ring had brought him here.
And in a ring lay his nemesis.

"The ring… the ring… the ring…" he repeated continuously, until his hips that had grown cold suddenly felt warmer.

As the warmth spread through his body, he realized its source. The realization jettisoned him out of his stupor, and he felt the stone floor under him. It was wet and warm.

Sitting at the bottom of the well, wet and alone, Aneni began to cry. His body shook, his neck stretched, his shoulder blades pulled, as he wailed helplessly.

The ring… the ring… his heart was beating erratically. It had forgotten its rhythm – for his life in this world would end soon – and he would never reach the afterlife.

Never.

〰〰 ۝۝۝ 〰〰

The city center looked beautiful tonight. Ironically, of the five roads that converged here, one that was no longer a road but a reedy street, was called the King's Road. The street was a leftover from the times of the past, when Thinis was the capital of Upper Egypt, which was then called *Ta-shema* or the land of the reeds. In those glorious days of Thinis, the road went straight up to the palace, and it was almost twice as broad as it was now. People traveled in litters or upon donkeys, and on both sides of the road grew palms and cactuses. One could almost see the Nile shimmering in distance.

But those were the days of the past. Now, the King's Road was a narrow street that twisted and wobbled between two rows of little rooms that appeared to be leaning inward into the street, thus blocking the rays of the sun from reaching it. While the street was always humming with activity, it transformed in to a riot of lights and colors when night fell. Tonight the street was busier as men, young and old alike, had poured into the city for the event of the century, and King's Road was a place that no man would want to give a miss.

The men who had gathered here hadn't brought along their wives, for in their opinion, it wasn't a sight a woman could stomach. The other reason was, of course, the women of King's Road.

But the women of King's Road were different from the wives they left at home. They were made of sterner stuff, and they had seen nearly everything, so their stomach didn't turn to water when they saw the impalements or the mutilation. For them, these were normal sights. They would go about their daily chores, fetching water or buying grocery, while a man lost his ears or his thumb for disloyalty or for stealing, or a woman her nose for bringing another man to her marital bed.

But tonight they too were excited. For one, the Burning would bring business to the city, and then also because most of them wanted to be there to witness the event of the century.

Khenmet was a woman of King's Road.

She lived down the road, away from the center, where the dregs of society weren't allowed. As the reedy street shimmied away from the center, it flared out and became broader. The tiny rooms gave way to bigger houses. Khenmet lived in one such house and owned a few of those stunted street-rooms, which she leased out to those young streetwalkers who couldn't afford to own one.

Right now, she was sitting on a *diwan,* leaning back upon one of the many cushions that surrounded her. Her house didn't look like much from the outside, for it was made of whitewashed fire-baked mud-bricks like all the other houses, but its interiors were richly done. One of her rich patrons had got her chambers paved with marble. Another had gifted her the carpet that covered the wall behind the *diwan*. There were many who had contributed to her bedchamber's décor and her jewels.

She was nothing without her patrons, and she knew it – and this knowledge had always helped her be content and happy.

But today she wasn't, for her thoughts just couldn't keep

still. She waved one of her maids to pour her some *sherbet*. Her maid, a young girl of about sixteen, poured her a combination of wine and pomegranate juice, and offered her the goblet.

Khenmet took a sip and nodded her approval.

"Are you worried about something?" the maid asked.

She shook her head and waved the maid away. They were becoming more audacious each passing day and their forwardness was her fault. Had she not been so lonely, she wouldn't have allowed them this impertinence, but a woman sometimes ached to hear a voice – and a woman in her circumstance, ached to hear the voice of another woman, and not of a man.

Not a man's voice. Especially not his!

The *sherbet* made her feel better, but her mind was still not at peace. She knew in her heart, that it would never be – not unless she did something about what she knew.

She knew something about the Burning that others did not.

And he had himself told her about it. He was drunk and somewhat incoherent when he had babbled, but she knew exactly what he had meant.

Khenmet gulped down the remaining *sherbet* and put the goblet aside. Then she forced herself to remember the details of that night. If she could do something to save an innocent, she would do it. *A love-priestess seldom got an opportunity to correct a wrong.*

She tried focusing on that night, a week ago, when he had stepped into her chambers swaying, his dark hair in disarray, his body strong and young, and his massive need unashamedly pushing against his *shenti*.

"Khenmet," he had called her name as he had lumbered to the bed and dropped upon it.

"Yes, my lord," she had answered, lifting his feet out of his sandals and placing them upon the bed.

"I want something…" he spoke haltingly, "something different, something…out-worldly – take me with you to *Duat.*"

Khenmet had tried to ignore his maunderings. He was

a rich client, a man who wanted and expected pleasure – and his expectations often went beyond the normal. If he wanted to experience *Duat* or the afterworld in her bed, she would try to please him the best she could.

She had stepped out of her gown and straddled him. Offering him her ample bosom and pushing their dark big aureoles toward him, she took his hand and placed it upon her breast. Despite his partial stupor, he squeezed it hard, making her squeal.

Whenever he visited her, she squealed and yelped, shrieked and howled, but she had never complained, as he was her most profitable customer. He was the one who kept her away from the low end of the street.

That night she had kept whimpering and screeching, more than she needed to, for she had learned that it helped him peak sooner. She had gone through the rut, moaning and gasping, groaning and howling, until she felt him erupt inside her. He had begun to snore moments after.

She got out of the bed carefully, as quietly as she could. She knew him well. After his siesta he would be back being the demon he was, more ferocious and a lot more cruel, but until he woke up, she knew that she could relax. So she slipped into her linen gown and went outside, into her antechamber, where she dropped upon her *diwan* and closed her eyes.

Khenmet had once been beautiful and her beauty had become her curse, for if she weren't beautiful, her tormentor would never have discovered her. The color of her skin was darker than gold but lighter than bronze, and her hair was as black as the kohl that she used in her eyes.

Her eyes still closed, she raised her hand to her forehead. Under the fringe of her hair, was the cut that he had given her. Half a finger long it started from her hairline and slipped into her brow. It was also the first in a long series of cuts and bruises that she would acquire over the years. Her other patrons had dwindled as the marks upon her face and body had grown, and that had made her dependent on the monster that lay in her bedchamber.

She was sitting there upon the *diwan* with just a wall separating her from the man who had butchered her face, when he had woken up. He flung the curtain aside and strode in naked, and turgid once again.

"Khenmet, my whore," he rumbled, "come to me. Let me in once again."

She followed him inside. Standing near the bed, she began unclipping the shoulder-clip to remove her gown.

He lunged at her and caught her hand.

"Don't remove it," he said, leering at her in an unreal way, suddenly filling her up with fear. In the flickering light of the torch, his face looked ugly. With his nostrils flared and his taut lips parted to reveal an unusually straight line of teeth, he looked like a demon from *Duat*. His larger than life shadow that was cast upon the wall behind had no neck and his shoulders looked even broader than they were.

He pulled her down upon the bed, making her lie supine. Then he arranged her hands at her sides and brought her feet together. When she looked at him and tried to speak, he clapped his hand upon her mouth. Then he moved his hand up and closed her eyes too.

"Shhh…" he whispered. "Don't see. Don't speak. Don't move. Play dead."

And so she lay under him as he pushed her gown up, revealing her thighs, and then slid his palm between her legs.

"Resist. Be rigid," he growled when she opened her legs too quickly. He pushed his hand between her clenched thighs, his ring abrading her skin, making her gasp and inciting him to hurt her more.

"Not a sound. I don't want to hear you breathe," he hissed. Then he had climbed upon her, touching her body in an odd way, like he was touching wood, he trailed his finger from her throat to the center of her chest, then slid his hand under the linen and found her breast. Squeezing it hard, he pulled back and positioned himself at top of her and entered her.

"Tighten up," he rasped again.

She kept her mouth closed, not allowing herself even the relief of a cry as he caused her pain, tearing inside her in an evil and unearthly frenzy, until she gave up and cried.

He suddenly went limp and slipped out. Her momentary relief whirled into a flurry of pain as he slapped her hard on her cheek, the metal of his ring cutting first into her cheek then her lips.

That was just the beginning. He had gone on slapping and beating her, until she had rolled off the bed and lay upon the carpet on her side, hugging her knees close to her chest and whimpering.

"I asked you for just one thing. Play dead. And you couldn't do that! Do I have to kill you first?" he had shouted at her, his mad fury making him slur his words. He had then downed a whole pitcher of beer, before starting again.

She had played the part of the dead. She hadn't squealed when he had kneaded and crushed her breasts; she had suffered in silence, when his ring had scoured the soft flesh of her thighs; and she hadn't let a single sigh escape her lips when he had pounded into her mercilessly, abrading her insides.

He had left immediately after.

She had lain on her bed, the way he had left her, for a long time. In a way, she had felt dead herself. She had been lying there, half naked, her eyes peeled to the roof, when her maid had knocked.

That night had been the worst of all nights that Khenmet had spent with him. She was a love-priestess, a woman who excelled at the craft of making love. She had taught the art of love to many, and she had herself practiced it to bring happiness to half the nobility of Thinis.

Tonight, when the whole Thinis was congregating at the city center to see the necrophile burn, Khemnet sat upon her *diwan* and remembered that night when Senitef had given her his last lesson in hatred.

The maid came in again.

"Do you want anything else?" She asked. Then she paused and added, somewhat sheepishly. "All the girls are going to the city center. The Burning…"

Khenmet interrupted and waved her away.

"Go, but return quickly, and stay safe. The travelers are a risky lot."

They were just young girls, trying to earn their livelihood. *They hadn't even learned to fear, let alone hate.*

After the maid left, Khenmet rose from her *diwan* and went inside her bedchamber. The bed was on her right. On the left was another door - one with a wooden panel that swung inwards. It was a new kind of door that one of her older and kinder patrons had gifted her.

She opened the door and entered into the small dark room beyond. This was where she kept her jewelry and clothes. It was an armoire with shelves, except that she could walk into it.

There was an oil lamp in a wall-sconce that could light up the space, but she didn't need light to find what she wanted. She felt under her linens. It was there, right where she had left it. She picked it up, carefully, almost reverentially, for it was a blessing from the gods. It would redeem not only her life, but also the afterlives of many dead women.

Khenmet came out into her bedchamber and sat down upon the edge of her bed. Then slowly, she opened her fist. There it was. The gold ring that had a circle with a tangent – it was the circle of eternal protection. The *shen*-ring protected its wearer and brought him fortune.

A smile spread upon her face.

He always wore the ring. At least in all the years that he had been visiting her, she had never seen him without it. She too knew the ring well for it had caused her pain. That night, it had broken the skin of her face when he had slapped her, then it had chaffed her thigh when he had tried to force open her *dead and rigid* thighs.

She had found it on her bed.

When she had heard about the man who had done the unthinkable, she had immediately recognized her cruel patron as the necrophile. Never in her years as a love-priestess, she had come across a man who wanted to make love to the dead. They had all wanted her alive – they wanted her vivacious and her lovemaking vigorous. Death excited him and the dead attracted him – and when he had first asked her to play dead, it was the night that the necrophile was caught.

She knew that she would never escape Senitef, neither in life, and now knowing him, nor in death.

But if he were to be burned, she would be free of him forever.

〰 ◊◊◊ 〰

It was already afternoon when Ita had left Lord Senitef's villa and started her walk back. Usually, she enjoyed this walk, but tonight each step she took was filled with fear.

Now that she was alone with nothing to distract her mind, everything that had happened since morning returned to her in vivid detail.

She had entered Lord Senitef's bedchamber upon Lady Senitef's insistence, and realized that Senitef had heard her conversation with his wife and was expecting her, for he was standing in the middle of the room with nothing on his body to hide the hideousness that emerged from under his belly. Naked,

Senitef looked every bit like the monster that he was. She knew that he had ravaged the souls of every housemaid in his household, the same as his father. Ever since she had left the kitchen and begun to work in the house, he had been making indecent advances toward her – a pinch, a grope, sometimes a slap. She had borne it without complaining, even though she knew where it was all going.

She could leave the job. Her father would be happy if she did, for his embalming business had been doing rather well these past years. She hadn't, only because Aneni worked there too, and she would have hated if Senitef had hurt him in any way.

But now Aneni was gone from the villa, and soon he would be gone from the world. There was no need for her to put up with Senitef anymore.

She turned to leave.

Senitef was prepared for her flight, so in two quick strides, he caught up with her, and dragged her back in.

"Why won't you have me? You aren't all that discerning, are you? Or that lover of the dead has turned you dead too?"

She stared at him in shocked silence. Her eyes were involuntarily drawn to his stele's red glare.

She forced herself to look away from the monster.

"Oh, does it shock you that I know?" he mocked her. "I've seen you in the granary and in the stores with him. I've watched you both in throes of pleasure, right there, on the floor – on *my* floor! I've wanted you for years! Why do you think I brought you here from the kitchen?"

Then, with the alacrity of a cobra, he lunged at her and pinning her hands behind her back, he pushed her toward the bed.

As he struggled to get her on the bed, she fought hard, doing all she could. She used her nails to rake his flesh, but that only seemed to excite him more – then she tried to thrust her knee between his legs, but his weight upon her made it impossible for her to maneuver her position.

Half her body was upon the bed and he had torn her linen shift off, when she heard the Mistress's voice.

"A week has gone by and you still haven't found your *shen*-ring. You must find it. It's your lucky ring and if…"

The curtains parted and Lady Senitef stepped into the room.

Senitef looked up and saw her, but he didn't release Ita. It was as if both he and his wife had been through similar situations before.

"Both of you, get up and get dressed," Lady Senitef instructed. Her voice unfazed by the indecency of the scene in front of her. Ita had risen from the bed and rushed out, still holding the end of her shift in her fist.

Outside in the living chambers, there was a deep lee where she could stand hidden from anyone who came in. She stood there silently for a few moments, allowing her breath to normalize.

Then she slipped down against the wall and sat there for a very long time. Quite oddly, a strange peace descended upon her, as for the first time in the last two days, she had stopped thinking about Aneni. What happened today had changed her focus.

She knew that she had lost her job. Lady Senitef would never let her set foot in her house anymore.

Ita didn't care. What she was worried about was her mother. Her mother could lose her job too.

As she pleated her shift and pinned it under her breasts, still dazed, she felt a hand upon her shoulder.

Ita flinched, scared that it might be Senitef, and turned.

"You love him a lot, don't you?" Lady Senitef asked, her voice soft and full of concern.

"Lord Senitef? No, my lady… I don't. I…" Ita stammered.

"Not him, girl. He cannot be loved. I don't know of anyone who has ever loved him. Not even his mother. I know because I've heard her praying for his death," Lady Senitef replied.

Ita looked at her molester's wife, her eyes wide with a mix of anxiety and curiosity.

"Ita," Lady Senitef smiled, "my husband has collected a large number of *friends* who would love to see him suffer for his sins, and who would like to help us."

"Help us?" Ita mumbled.

"Don't repeat everything I say. I know that you are scared, but don't fear me. I am on your side," said Lady Senitef, as she pulled Ita out of her hiding place. "Come with me. I want you to meet someone."

Ita followed Lady Senitef into her bedchamber. She had never seen her mistress receive anyone in her bedchamber before, so it was obvious to her that this meeting was going to be a private one.

"Don't breathe a word about this to anyone," Lady Senitef whispered, as she motioned her to sit down.

Ita nodded her head and sat down upon a cushion on the floor. Lady Senitef's bedchamber was a magnificent room with large windows and plenty of light. Her bed was covered with the softest linen that could be found anywhere in Egypt and her feather-pillows were encased in silk. Her *ankh*-table too was gilded in gold. It was a rich noblewoman's room, and while Ita had tidied it up many times, this was the first time that she was sitting in it.

Lady Senitef's guest who sat in a chair, looked upon her with curiosity.

"So you are Ita. The girl who has our Lord Senitef in her thralls," she observed. Her voice, Ita noticed, was soft and sweet, unlike her mistress's. The woman skin was the color of honey and her eyes were the deepest shade of black, like they were made of onyx. And yet, to mar her beauty a scar rose from her brow and ran across her forehead. But what she couldn't help noticing was the blue lily with three lapis lazuli petals that shone upon her wig, proclaiming that she was a love priestess.

Ita averted her eyes. She didn't want to appear gawking.

"She knows my husband better than I do. He spends more nights at her place than at home," said Lady Senitef, her voice oddly calm, almost indifferent and devoid of any bitterness that a wife would normally feel upon meeting a woman who slept with her husband.

"What is your name?" Ita asked hesitatingly.

The woman with the beautiful but scarred face laughed gently.

"My name isn't important, Ita. But what I have brought is," she said in her sweet calming voice, and opened her fist.

Lord Senitef's *shen*-ring sat snug in the middle of her palm.

ᨃᨃᨃ ۝۝۝ ᨃᨃᨃ

Ita left the villa running. She had never run this fast – not ever.

The mystery of Senitef's missing *shen*-ring had resolved. Both of them, Lady Senitef and the love priestess, who wouldn't tell Ita her name, knew the real necrophile. They had slept with him for years, and they were both sure that he was the one.

This could only mean one thing. Her Aneni was wrongly implicated, and if she could gather evidence, she could save him, and save her own life and sanity.

They all wanted out.

Lady Senitef,

The love priestess,
And she!

They had done their bit. Now it was her turn, and she had to play it right.

She was the only one who could change all their fates!

Ita had run back the whole way. She had leaped over boulders and even cut her way short by running through the farms and being shouted at by the owners. It was as if she had grown wings - wings of hope. Time was of essence. Everything had to be done quickly, and she needed to enlist her father's help if her plan were to succeed. So she ran up the steps of her father's embalming chamber where her father and two of his apprentices were busy preparing two new bodies for the salt bath.

She slowly walked to her father and placed her head upon his shoulder.

"Father," she said, "I need your help."

"Don't you see, I am working," he scolded her. He always did, but she knew that he doted upon her. He told her to wait outside and joined her after washing his hands.

"Yes?" he asked. He was a man of few words, and recently, since Aneni's conviction, he had almost stopped talking to his daughter. She had chosen Aneni to be his son-in-law, and he had found it difficult to forgive her lapse of judgment.

"Father, I found this when I was cleaning the embalming chamber this morning. I know that it belongs to Lord Senitef," she said softly, holding the *shen*-ring upon her palm for her father to see.

She had never lied to her father before, but telling a lie that could save an innocent life was a deed that had the blessing of gods.

"Lord Senitef is a respectable man who has no reason to be in our embalming chamber," her father said. "Are you sure that this is his ring?"

Ita turned the ring over, showing him the hieroglyphs

etched on its underside. Her father had some hieroglyphic training, enough for him to read the name.

"What does that prove? Only that he was in the embalming chamber. It doesn't tell us when, nor why," her father, the inveterate logician, reasoned.

"No Father," she said slowly, "it doesn't. Just the same as Aneni's being seen leaving the embalming chamber that evening, doesn't prove that he was responsible for… that abominable crime. At least he had an excuse to be there – he may have gone there looking for me, or to meet you, but Lord Senitef's ring has an even lesser reason to be found in the embalming chamber."

"Lord Senitef himself was one of the men who saw Aneni leave," her father reminded her.

"Yes, he was, Father."

Then she told him about her misadventure with Senitef that morning. She knew that it would make him angry. Unfortunately, the royalty, the nobility, and the rich; in that order, couldn't be touched by the commoners. She saw her father's nostrils flare and his lips tighten upon his teeth – he was angry.

"He should be the one burning – that ball of filth," her father stood up and started pacing, his eyes raining fire.

"Father, I have a plan. Will you help me mend my life?"

ᗯᗯᗯ 𓏏𓏏𓏏 ᗯᗯᗯ

On the morning of the execution, the prisoner was walked to the city-center in chains. It was a long walk, especially with the weight of the heavy metal shackles that were tied around his feet.

The crowd had spilled out of the city-center into the four colorless roads and the lone vibrant street. They had been waiting for the most evil criminal of the last hundred years to be burned alive, and so when they finally laid their eyes upon him, they went berserk.

The crowd, he thought, *was an odd beast.* It followed anything and anyone. It was like a gaggle of goose-chicks that upon hatching would start following the first thing that moved.

So when someone threw a stone, they followed. The stones came sailing through the air, scattering around him. Then someone else called him a name and the crowd followed again. Chants began to fill up the air – they sounded like a song of farewell to him. He closed his eyes and listened. They were extolling his virtues and praising him for going where no other man had gone before.

Desecrator.

Defiler.

Pervert.

Blasphemer.

They hated and envied him in the same breath. He didn't blame them for he knew that if he wasn't the one being executed today, he could have easily chanted the same words himself.

But they didn't know, did they?

They didn't know what delights were there to sample in the world of the dead. They were oblivious of what it felt like to step across into the afterlife and then step back into the land of living. Many in the crowd, who were here to denounce and denigrate him today, had barely touched the living flesh.

What would they know of the dead?

They knew nothing, he thought and smiled, when a stone hit his brow.

He raised his hand and touched his forehead. The stone had split the skin and blood was beginning to ooze out. He touched the blood with his fingers and looked at them. They were slick with red blood – his blood. The dead didn't bleed red. They bled black. He didn't fear death, for he had loved many who had gone to the other side. They didn't care.

The dead had no hatred left in them, unlike the living.

The living hated him. He had seen repulsion in their eyes. He had seen it in the distrustful eyes of his wife, whose eternity was bound to his; in the fearful eyes of his slave-girls, who were meant to please him; in the dark eyes of that wench Khenmet, who he had showered with gifts. He had even seen it in the eyes of his mother, who had learned of his ways with the dead by overhearing a conversation she wasn't meant to hear. Whenever he happened to be in her presence, he could see his mother's revulsion for him as she would quickly look away and begin clutching the many amulets that hung around her scrawny, bony neck, which had snapped rather quickly when his fingers had closed around it.

He knew the character of the rabble. After the spectacle, they would talk about him for a few days or even several weeks, and then they would stop. Decades later, the next generation of Egyptians would talk about him in hushed tones for he would have become a legend – an evil legend perhaps, yet a legend.

But that was the rabble.

In a way he was glad for being caught, for had it not been so, he would have died a normal, everyday death, and the only good thing they shall find to say about him was that his teeth were perfect.

Perfect teeth were the summary of all that the living found good in him. They never mentioned that he was big. More than a cubit taller than the tallest men in Egypt, and that he was strong. They feared him, but they never said anything. Nobody other than his wife had the courage to mention it to him. But that woman, may her body rot and fester, had told him why.

"You are a monster, blind to the pain of others. You revel in your own pleasure, caring little for the tears and gashes you inflict upon me," she had told him amidst tears. "That thing," she had pointed a finger at his pride, the one that his parents wanted him to keep hidden, which had made them call him *Akh-Min* or *Min*'s brother, "is evil forged into a weapon that destroys innocence, and you've used it to kill my soul."

Since then, she hadn't come to him. He too had ignored her, for the wenches were more accommodating and the dead were a lot more welcoming. They didn't think that he was a monster, nor did they weep and wail. They didn't try to shame him by talking about *Min* and his monstrous member.

His hands itched under the handcuffs. The sun was rising higher in the sky. Soon it would be noon. The crowd too was regaining its composure. The excitement of the first sighting had evaporated now. The Burning would take place after the Magistrate read out the *Ma'at* order in public. The vendors of fruits and water and beer were beginning to hawk their merchandize as the crowd had now grown tired and was in need of refreshments.

He felt agitated by the declining interest. He was still alive – these last few moments of his life had to be acknowledged and celebrated.

"You don't know," he shouted, "you don't know anything. The bond between the dead and the living is strong."

The crowd jeered and the necrophile leered.

We are the same, he thought, *at the subliminal level, just the same. We want to be accepted, regarded, respected, and praised.*

"You gave up looking for it," he screamed, "I found what you and I both wanted, because I dared to look for it where you won't."

He didn't see their faces.

He didn't care.

But they were all there - Khenmet and Ita and Aneni, and hidden behind the curtains of a litter, Lady Senitef.

∿∿ 𓏤𓏤𓏤 ∿∿

The evening before Senitef the necrophile was burned, had been a busy one for Ita and her family.

It had all started when Ita's mother had come out of their house screaming that Ita had consumed poison. Her father and his assistant had rushed to the house, and found Ita dead.

The embalming community was a small one and they were all very close – almost like family members. After the initial mourning, her father announced that her body would be taken to the embalming chamber, where it would remain the whole night. The ceremonies would begin the next morning. Her mother had insisted on sending a boy to the villa and informing Lady Intef about Ita's suicide.

"She must be informed. Ita had worked with her for so many years," her mother had explained.

All their relatives and neighbors had gathered at her father's house. When they took her body to the embalming chamber, her father was grieving, her friends crying, and her mother was beating her chest. The family was devastated.

The oldest woman in the neighborhood had voluntarily taken the responsibility of explaining Ita's death to everyone who arrived to console the grieving family.

"She was in love with that boy. What else could the poor soul do?" she would begin by telling the new arrival.

"Which boy?" they would ask, even the ones who knew. The rumormongers were forever ready to sample the grapevine.

"The one they are going to burn tomorrow," the old woman would then offer the juicier tidbit.

"How terrible," the visitors would then tut-tut their sympathy; shed an invisible tear or two for the dead girl, and leave. Before the night had deepened, everyone had learned about the misfortune that had befallen the embalmer's family.

Her father had one of the embalming stations cleaned and ready for her to use. She was laid down, wearing a pleated gown the color of honey and with lilies woven in her hair.

They had stayed for a while, reciting prayers that would keep her body safe from evil spirits, then after lighting seven lamps around her, they had left. Her father had been the last one to leave. He had held her hand for a few moments before leaving, and told her that they would be right outside, and that there was nothing to fear.

The dead spent their first night alone or in the company of the other dead. Around her were three more, who had already been eviscerated.

Nothing happened for a rather long time. *What if Lady Senitef and the love-priestess were both wrong in their assessment?* She thought. They would burn Aneni then, and Senitef would rape her with a vengeance, especially if he learned about how her death was a bait to bring him out.

The stone platform was cold and she wore only a thin linen gown. Her bladder was filling up and she wanted to get up to go, but this was her only chance, and she couldn't lose it. So she lay, trying to keep her attention away from the tension developing in her bladder.

Her concentration was broken by the slow creak of the door opening. Lying there with her eyes closed and her face stony, she tried to reason it out. It couldn't be anyone but him for why would anyone else open the door so softly – *like a thief?*

It had to be him.

She heard the footsteps approaching, heavy and quick, and then he was close enough for her to hear and smell his breath. She had smelled it just that morning. Her heart began racing, faster than the fastest galley in the Nile boat race. She wondered if her eyes moved or her expression changed and hoped that it hadn't. She tried to become one with the stone that she lay upon. She had to appear dead, but he knew the dead so well.

What if he didn't fall for the ruse?

Then she heard his breath come faster, and she felt his big broad hand upon her throat.

Is he going to kill me? She thought frantically. *Why weren't they coming in?*

The answer was simple. They were waiting to catch him red-handed. *Would it mean that she would have to subject herself to the whole act?*

Oh god, she prayed, *help me.*

Then she heard his gruff voice in her ear.

"You wanted me to take you the way I like it best, didn't you? And so you died. You died for me," he chuckled.

She kept still, afraid that her expression might've changed, or her eyes under her lids may have moved. She felt grateful for the small flickering flames of the earthen lamps.

And then she felt his body upon her. His hand caressing her thighs, before he softly moved her gown up, and pushed his palm between her legs.

The door burst open and they poured in. All the embalmers, her father, mother, uncles, cousins, even the neighbors.

In that moment, the witnesses also became the captors. They caught and tied him with papyrus ropes, while Ita's mother helped her down and pulled a linen shawl around her shoulders.

The violator of the dead, however, was nonplussed. After his initial shock had passed, he had stopped caring.

They sent the news to the Governor's office and also to the villa.

His wife came on a faster litter that was carried by four men instead of two. She had marched right up to him and slapped him on his face.

"For how many years have you been doing this?" she had asked him, her face twisted with hatred and revulsion.

A grin broke upon his face and went widening until he was thrown into a fit of laughter. When he stopped, he raised his eyes to look at her.

"Since I was twelve," he answered, saliva dripping out of the corner of his mouth.

Lady Senitef had run out of the room and thrown up on the steps. Inside, his raucous laughter had continued unabated.

ᨆᨆ ᨉᨉᨉ ᨆᨆ

The Burning had evoked a mixed response from the crowd. The stench of it was unbearable, but the flaming specter that ran about in the cage, screaming in agony, gave them what they needed. Solace to some, and entertainment to others, who had come here in the hope of seeing something that they could talk about for years to come.

The crowd didn't know that among them were those whose lives were touched by the man whose burning they had come to watch.

The necrophile's wife hadn't stepped out of her litter, which stood among several others that had lined up against the sides of the four streets. She had stayed inside, listening to the jeers of the crowd and the screams of the man who had fathered her children. She prayed to her gods so that her children may not take after their father.

Khenmet too was there. She was among those who had spent the morning in the special court that had assembled to assess the new evidence and hear the witnesses. When the magistrate had called for witnesses other than the thirty-three who had caught Senitef in his abominable act, she had provided the colorful details of her own encounters with him. Now she had been given the opportunity to stand among the witnesses close to the execution square. As the crowd had cheered the witnesses and jeered at the necrophile, she had seen many pairs of eyes rest upon her. It was all good publicity for her business.

Aneni, who was still very weak and found it difficult to walk without support, was there too. The man who had implicated him in a crime so terrible that its punishment required the complete annihilation of a man's identity, in this life and the afterlife, deserved a death by fire. Aneni was glad that he was alive and hopeful that his reputation would be restored.

Ita had come to the Burning not to watch the necrophile go up in flames but to be with Aneni.

"Why did they take you away?" she asked, stealing her hand into his.

"Lord Senitef had raised the alarm. He said that he had seen me slink out of the embalming chamber the night it all happened."

"But why?" she asked, perplexed.

"Because I had seen him leave the embalming chamber," he replied. "He must have done it because he wanted you for himself."

"Yes," she whispered.

"When did you realize that I was innocent?" he asked.

"What?" she asked, distracted by a sudden commotion. The specter had collapsed on the floor of the execution square and he was now burning in a heap. She wondered if he had fainted or whether he still could feel the pain.

"How did you know that I was innocent?" he repeated his question.

"I didn't," she said, suddenly realizing that she had said something unexpected. "I always knew in my heart that you were innocent, but what I actually discovered was that…Senitef was the necrophile," she said feeling a strange squeeze upon her heart. She turned and looked at Aneni.

"I should have not lost heart. I should have remembered that I shall always have you on my side," he drew her close and smiled at her.

The momentary disquiet she had felt disappeared as a warm glow of love washed over her.

Her Aneni — her sweet, innocent Aneni was now with her. They will help each forget the nightmare and begin a new life. Now, neither she nor Aneni had to fear Senitef, for he was gone — both from this life and the afterlife.

ᗧᗧᗧ ◖◖◖ ᗧᗧᗧ

A week had passed since the Burning, but Ita still found it difficult to sleep. The burning man, running from one side of the cage to another, stumbling and falling, screaming and crying, invaded her dreams every night. The stench of the burning flesh assailed her nostrils, making it difficult for her to breathe. It woke her up gasping and sweating, clawing at the air around her.

Something wasn't right.

She didn't know what, but there remained a niggling doubt, which didn't allow her to forget those images.

That Burning, the one that they had witnessed a week ago, was seared in her memories for a reason — a reason that evaded her.

Why?

The defiler of the dead was burned. Gone forever.

What made her so anxious then?

It was the eleventh day after the Burning, the first day of the new ten-day week, and they were all trying to bring their lives back to normal.

This morning her father had asked her to clean out the armoires and the chest of drawers in the embalming chamber.

"And lock it before you leave," he had instructed, handing her a lock and a key. It appeared to be an interesting contraption made of bronze. Her father had got it made to keep the embalming chamber secure, for people were beginning to talk about letting the bodies of their young women relatives rot before they sent them for mummification.

The necrophile had ruined not only her peace but also her father's business.

Ita had gone to the embalming chamber in the afternoon.

The armoires were used to store the linen-bandages, and they were quite easy to organize. As she checked them one after the other, she also made a quick inventory of the skeins of bandages that were there. It was clear that the last two weeks had taken a toll on her father's work. He had neglected to order bandages for the mummies that would be ready for binding in another week from now.

She made a note to talk to her father about it. Then she attended to the cupboard that was used to store leather aprons and the material used to clean the embalming tables. Everything appeared to be in order there too.

Now, only the chest of drawers remained. After she was done with it, she would go to Aneni's house and meet him there.

ᵚᵛᵛ ๏๏๏ ᵚᵛᵛ

Ita hadn't gone to meet Aneni that evening. Instead she had sent a message to him.

She would meet him on her own turf.

She stood near the drawer where she had found the

ring with her name on it. Her thoughts muddied, in a distant corner of her mind, a hope still alive that he would have an explanation for it. She couldn't bear to think that she had lain with the defiler, and loved him enough to save him.

It was the bottom drawer that had yielded the ring.

His ring - the ring that she had given to him – the ring that he had promised never to take off – the ring that had her name on it!

The ring had no reason to be in that unused drawer that didn't open unless coaxed and cajoled. But it had answered a question that had been burning within her, consuming her peace and destroying her ability to be happy.

She knew that Senitef was guilty, but how did Senitef's guilt prove Aneni's innocence?

Was it because Senitef had implicated Aneni?

Or because Senitef had a motive – he wanted Ita for himself, and he had found an easy way to rid himself of Aneni?

She was expecting him. And yet when she heard his voice behind her, her blood turned to water. It was the same voice that set her heart aflutter, but tonight, it made her tremble with fear.

"What have you found?" Aneni asked. He was still playing his game, but slipping. If he knew enough to ask her that, he knew what it was.

She turned slowly and opened her palm, fear and disgust writ large upon her features.

Aneni looked at the ring, and a smile crept upon his lips.

He was cracking, the way Senitef had.

"I would have removed it, had your father not started locking the embalming chamber," he said, his smile deepening.

Ita looked at him in horror. He was confessing, *but why?*

She looked at him, her eyes sliding down to his hands – the hands that had touched her. She wanted to throw up, but his eyes had her pinned down. In face of her emotional turmoil, she had lost her will to act.

"It was you that day?" she asked, her voice shaking.

"That day? Yes. But the day before, it was him," he replied. "We were childhood friends. Together we had discovered the joy of lying with the dead. We were alike in many ways but different in one – he could be very careless. I, on the other hand, was excessively careful with everything, including the ring. I would put it in the drawer, because losing it under the dead could have been disastrous. I lost track of time - that was my mistake. They didn't see me getting out the first time – only when I had returned to fetch the ring that I had forgotten to take along. I should have left it there and nobody would have discovered it. You didn't, for six months. Senitef's resolve always weakened when he was with Khenmet. That woman had a strange hold upon him. I had warned him against it, but he had lost control. It happens sometimes, especially when you are easily swayed. It's one thing to lie with the dead and another to become obsessed with them. When that happens, they take control of your senses and make you do things that a rational man wouldn't do otherwise," he said calmly, hitching himself upon one of the embalming tables, where a body lay draining. He looked at it and added, "the dead slowly nibble at your rationality – leaving it porous and weak – allowing your two realities to mix."

"You are mad," she spat.

"I am not. I am rational, and I will always be. The wells of the living dead where they hold you when you await your execution – that's where even the strongest minds lose their capability to think – and I returned unscathed. I have a very strong mind, Ita."

Ita turned her face away. She couldn't bear to look at him.

"Have you ever looked at yourself, Ita?" he asked.

She didn't respond. She didn't want to talk to him anymore.

"Let us be honest. You aren't beautiful. Khenmet, even with that hideous scar on her face is far more attractive than you are. Your attraction, limited as it is, exists only because you are young, and your youth will soon fade away. You aren't rich either. Why then, do I want to marry you?"

"Because I am an embalmer's daughter?" she asked, haltingly. A faint impression of a thought that he could have once hurt her by his unkind words crossed her mind.

"Yes, and also because you are intelligent. And this is why, I believe, that you will appreciate the offer I am about to make. Marry me. Let my secrets become yours. Give me my paradise, and I will give you your life."

Ita didn't answer.

"Or I must kill you and go away. Start my life somewhere else – as an embalmer's apprentice perhaps. I know you love me, Ita, so why won't you help me in my quest for happiness?"

He frightened her; but she wouldn't run.

She knew that today she had finally gained her freedom. Her hatred for him had sliced away all that had bound her to him. When he was gone, she would feel nothing for him – she would carve out the years she wasted with the monster, feed them to the Nile crocodiles, and start afresh.

"So what is it going to be?" he asked, bringing his right hand forward, in which he held a cutting knife that he had picked up from the tools-table while coming in.

"I don't love you," she screamed and lunged at him with the black blade of her great grandfather's obsidian knife. Its blade was as sharp in her hour of need as it was when her ancestor had used it to slit open the sides of the deceased to divest them of their entrails.

She plunged it into his side and dragged it down. It cut through his skin, smooth and soft, like it was slicing through a slab of butter.

He crumbled upon the floor in a heap.

ᴡᴡᴡ ꝺꝺꝺ ᴡᴡᴡ

That afternoon, another Burning took place. A fire blazed on the distant horizon – the smell of the roasting flesh was quickly dispersed through the air that was blowing away from the city.

The ring sat at the bottom of Nile, forever.

ᴡᴡᴡ ꝺꝺꝺ ᴡᴡᴡ

Historical Notes:

Herodotus, the Greek Historian who lived in the fifth century B.C. has written about the embalming practices in Ancient Egypt.

According to Herodotus, the bodies of the wives of high officials and rich men weren't sent for embalming, until three to four days had passed after their death. This was to save their bodies from being defiled by necrophiles.

Herodotus mentions a case of necrophilia, where the necrophile was discovered with some help from a fellow workman.

Nubkaure Amenemhat II was the third pharaoh of the 12th Dynasty of Ancient Egypt. He lived and ruled around 1900 BC.

Ma'at was the ancient Egyptian goddess of truth and justice.

THE BREWERESS OF OMBO

~ | Ptolemaic Egypt | ~

THE BREWERESS OF OMBO

It was dusk already when the breweress received news from Alexandria. Cleopatra was dead. The turmoil was great and Egypt was in pain, but the greatest agent of this pain, thought the breweress, was Cleopatra herself. Egypt had lost its last Pharaoh. The *Nekhbet* of Upper Egypt and the *Uraeus* of the Lower will no longer grace the brow of Egypt's rulers, and yet, it was now all going to be better – at least for the common Egyptian, for the embers of strife that had torn Egypt apart for the last five decades, were already dying.

The brewery had three main sections - the silos that stored barley, oat, and emmer, the sheds where the beer was processed, and the shop from where it was sold. Right now, only the shop was open. This was the time when people stopped by the shop to get their beer flasks filled before they headed home, and so the counter was busy. The coins with Cleopatra's face stamped upon them were still in circulation, along with the coins that had the visage of the earlier Ptolemaic rulers.

The barter system that the Egyptians had used earlier

was a disgrace. How could a nation so civilized otherwise sustain its economy through barter was something that the breweress had always found unimaginable. She sat upon a low *diwan* in her chamber at the back of the shop counting *drachmas*. Life was good. From a materialist's viewpoint, it wasn't as good as it was before, but the breweress had long since developed a spiritual way of looking at life. She now had peace. She also had Helios, who was better than her two previous paramours, both in bed and in temperament.

There isn't any need left to pretend anymore, she sighed.

One of the boys from the shop parted the curtain that separated her chamber from the shop and peeped in.

"Lady Hera," he curtsied. "The last customer has left."

"Close the shop," she instructed the boy. Then she carefully got off the *diwan*, and slid her feet into her papyrus sandals that lay upon the packed mud floor.

The boy left, and a middle-aged man entered.

"The news from north is terrible," he said.

Hera lifted her eyes and looked into his. Her eyes were captivating, even arresting. They could make a man feel like he owned the world.

"The double-crown has gone missing," he said, "and Octavian has sent his fleet up the Nile."

"Yes," mused the breweress, "the double-crown has gone missing, forever. And it might be a good thing for Egypt."

"They say the streets of Alexandria are filled with the cries *of Long Live Cleopatra.*"

"Are they?" she asked, perfunctorily.

It didn't sway her the least. She couldn't care less. She was a breweress, and she was going to remain one all her life, she thought.

Hera bent down to shut the lid of the box of *drachmas*, which contained their earnings of the day. Then she stood up straight and adjusted the pleats of her gown. She hated her body nowadays. It was beginning to spill out of its hourglass shape and settle into the folds of her linen gown. Bearing four children could wreak havoc on a woman's body. She was almost forty and by the grace of *Hathor*, her red flower still blossomed every month unerringly.

She would love to have another child, not only because she missed her other four, but also because nothing made a family appear more normal than a brood.

"Helios," she whispered, her lips poised to blow out the last candle in the room, "all I hope is that they give her a decent burial. We don't want her *ka* haunting our beloved new Emperor, do we?"

Through her wry smile, Helios saw her mask slip for a moment. He wrapped his arms around her and drew her close into his embrace. He loved her, more than anyone else in the world. He had followed her everywhere, shared every secret of hers. Since she was fifteen, he had sworn to keep her safe.

He shall keep his promise.

᠁ ᠔᠔᠔ ᠁

Cleopatra palace was beautiful. Each of her ancestors had added something to the palace that was built for Ptolemy the First when Alexander had left him behind to govern Egypt. That was nearly three hundred years ago. For three centuries Alexandria had stood upon an island on the mouth of the Nile delta, proud of its Greek heritage, inviting the scholars and the traders of the world in, while keeping the enemies out.

The palace was right in the middle, fortified first by the city that was built around it and then by the intermingling waters of the Nile and the ocean. The floor of the palace was marble, cool in the summer afternoons when Sun's rays beat upon Alexandria. Its walls were made of etched and painted limestone, and the massive pillars that held up the heavy stone roof, were made of polished pink granite.

In the covered *verandah* that overlooked the central court of the palace, Cleopatra lay upon a gilded, painted *diwan* made of cedar wood. Charmion sat near her, while Iras poured her pomegranate juice in a silver goblet. Charmion and Iras were her favorite companions. They were her handmaidens, her shadows, as many called them, for they never left her alone. Menas the eunuch sat upon a low stool at the foot of the *diwan*.

The prisoner's screams of anguish rang out in the court as Iras held out the goblet for Cleopatra.

"What snake is that?" she enquired, taking the goblet, and raising herself on her elbow to get a better view of the scene.

In the middle of the court, a man in dirty rags was rolling on the floor of a cage. He appeared to be in great pain. The mesh of the cage was fine enough to contain the snake, which had been dropped inside by the snake handler. After biting the man, the brown snake that was barely a cubit long, had slithered in the corner. The man was clutching his left arm, which had begun to swell, and crying in pain.

"Your Highness, it's the horned viper," cooed Menas in his sweet singsong voice that had never broken into the bass of a man's.

Cleopatra squinted her eyes. There indeed were two tiny horns on the snake's head.

"I hear that its poison isn't always fatal," she mused.

Menas rolled the end of his purple linen shawl about his index finger, and then whispered, "The horned viper is an excellent weapon against the enemies you hate."

"And so, Menas," Cleopatra leaned forward pinning him down with her eyes, "you brought it for me. Am I your enemy?"

"But," Menas spluttered, his eyes turning round and bulging, like a beetle's, "you said, all snakes."

"Remove this one and show me the next," she waved him away. Menas rose, pushing his knees down with his palms. His portly body ensconced in layers of differently colored linen made him look like a huge colored boulder. He was fond of his food, and that had been his biggest failing. But recently, it wasn't just his weight that had been bothering him. It was also his need to urinate more frequently.

Cleopatra took a sip of her drink. The ragged man, her experimental subject, had begun to bleed from his arm, which had now swollen up like a goat's bladder. This wasn't the way she wanted to die. She didn't want to die in pain. She needed a poison that felt like a mother's embrace and would softly put her to sleep. She prayed it wouldn't come to that, but she liked to be prepared.

When the next cage was wheeled in, the cries of the man in the first cage that was being taken away could still be heard.

If only it were Octavian in that cage, she thought. *But would it really change things?* Rome won't be deterred. In Rome, there were many who would gladly usurp her dear Egypt, and Octavian's death would merely make them bay for her blood louder. It wasn't the solution.

Cleopatra tried to concentrate on the experiment. This man was younger and more robust, and he looked a little like Apollodorus. Reminded of him, she turned to Charmion.

"Go and check if there's a scroll from Apollo," she sent her away to the administrative block. Apollo was away on a secret mission. If all the pieces fell in their right places, the plan would be a success, and yet it was impossible to change what *Shayt*, the goddess of fortune and destiny, was planning for her. *If only, for once in all these years, Shayt would help her plans instead of thwarting them!*

"Your Highness, witness the Egyptian Cobra," Menas climbed the steps back up and settled upon his cushioned stool.

She handed her empty tumbler to Ira and focused on the new cage. The man inside was strong and tall and his face was turned toward her. He looked at her through the mesh and when their eyes met, he entreated her to set him free.

"Great Egypt, I've three little children at home and my wife is waiting for me to return. I am a farmer. At least allow me a trial," he beseeched, attempting to stop his tears from rolling down his cheeks.

She heard his plea and thought why it didn't tug at her heartstrings. A faint memory of a little girl hopping down from her litter to nurse the wound of a child that had fallen and hurt its knee flitted across her mind. That girl, the young Cleopatra, whose heart would melt when she saw someone in pain, had died long ago. Her heart had now turned to stone – *all these years, all the things that she had done* – she couldn't be that girl with a heart that wept for others.

"Bring out the snake," she said to Menas, who raised his arm to signal. He wore rings on all his fingers - ten stones to ward off ten different kinds of evils. *What if there were more?*

The handler slid the plate that covered the hole on top of the mesh aside, and allowed the snake to slither out of the papyrus basket into the cage. The snake was almost as long as his prey was tall.

Cleopatra watched fascinated. Her eyes as arresting as the cobra's, outlined with black galena, her lids painted green; her lips luscious from distance, the red ochre carefully expanding and plumping her thinning lips; her wig with gold bells woven in it carefully perched upon her head; she watched the snake approach its prey.

She wasn't being watched herself, but she was painfully aware of the fact that she too was prey, and so was her son. Rome hadn't let them out of her sight since the death of Caesar.

She remembered telling her son a week ago, the last time she had set her eyes upon him, that there were two kinds of people in the world – the predators and the prey. And everyone had to choose between being one of the two. The prey had the wide innocent eyes of a victim, and the predators had thin slit eyes that saw everything and anticipated every move of their foe. She had asked her son Caesarion to be the latter, but in her heart of stone was another smaller and softer heart that beat for her children, and it kept reminding her that Caesarion too had wide innocent eyes – his eyes made her anxious all the time, waking her up in the middle of the night, making her pray fervently to *Shayt,* asking her to keep her son safe.

"Majesty?" Menas's voice dragged her back to the present. She swung her feet down to find her gold-encrusted, gem-studded leather slippers. She wanted to see this up close.

The snake moved like a poem, soft and swift, and raised his hood. The condemned man was standing with his back against the mesh, pressing into it to draw himself away from the snake. In the confines of the small cage, however, the distance between them was not more than a couple of paces, which was nothing for an Egyptian cobra. It reared its head and shot across the cage, striking the man straight on his chest. The man watched in horror as the snake's fangs pierced his skin and deposited the snake's paralyzing venom into him – then, realizing the finality of it, he closed his eyes and screamed.

Cleopatra had read about the symptoms of a cobra's bite. Now she was witnessing them. Clutching his chest, the bitten man flopped down upon the floor of the cage. She knew that at first the pain would be local, but then very quickly it would spread through his body, giving him a terrible headache. This would be followed by unbearable abdominal cramps and convulsions that would make his muscles spasm uncontrollably. Finally, mercifully, he would stop breathing.

She watched, mesmerized, until he once again turned to face her, his face contorted and his eyes screwed in pain. He was beginning to froth from the mouth. Before she could fathom his intention, he hurled a gurgling curse upon her.

"*O' Amun*, may this witch never see her children again," he shouted, before doubling over in pain as the convulsions and the headache took over.

Cleopatra averted her eyes. She didn't believe in curses, and yet, a cloud of darkness descended upon her. She clutched the pendant of *Hathor* that lay upon her breast and prayed for the safety of Caesarion.

She stood there with her eyes closed, listening to the cries of the dying man, until she felt a soft hand upon her shoulders.

"Majesty, I checked. No scroll came in today," Charmion informed, "but he is waiting for you in your chambers."

〰 ◊◊◊ 〰

While Cleopatra was holding her snake trials in Alexandria, about a hundred leagues south from her, in Ombo, a brewer and his family had just sold their brewery.

The city of Ombo was a peaceful place. It wasn't a large city by any means, but the beer business here was brisk. It may have been because of its past as a garrison town, or because beer was more than a drink here – it was a way for the locals to meet and connect, to share stories and anecdotes, for Ombo was situated in the south of Egypt, a long distance away from the delta, and the pace of life was rather slow, even in the heart of the city.

The Dew Day Brewery was a mid-sized establishment, located slightly away from the city center. The slaves and the servants ran the brewery quite well and there was hardly an occasion when anyone had to meet the owners, so the patrons had no idea that the brewery was being sold, and that soon the management of the brewery would change hands.

The current owners of the brewery had signed the title-deed scroll and transferred the rights to Hera and Helios, a couple from the delta who were looking to move south. Mehy, a friend of the brewer's wife from her youth, had got the deal struck.

The brewer's wife was from the north. She had grown up in Memphis, and the thought of going back after thirty long years excited her. The brewery that they were taking over in Memphis was new, but the brewer and his wife were sure that soon it would be doing good business. After all, Memphis was a city bigger and richer than Ombo, and then, Memphis had a different appeal. Situated right next to the biggest and the oldest necropolis of Egypt, the city was imbued with a hint of mysticism. It thronged with Egyptians and foreigners alike. They came there in search of contentment, happiness, even pleasure, and a floating population was a lot more conducive to businesses such as theirs.

The brewer and his wife had given it a lot of thought, and eventually made the decision to move.

They were to board the galley that left early next morning. Their things were packed, and they would all be sleeping in the big hall tonight. The brewers had four children, the eldest was nearing seventeen now. The floor in their living quarters was marble, unlike in the shop where it was just packed-mud. The brewer's father had trained him well and so he knew that there wasn't a point in spoiling the workers by making them accustomed to luxuries above their station.

The brewer and his son unrolled the mattresses on the floor while the breweress ticked items off the papyrus scroll she held in her hand.

"We've packed everything that we must carry along," she quipped. Just to fill the silence with words.

"Have we heard from the new owners? When are they

moving in?" the son asked.

"Perhaps in a month. In the meantime, Mehy will be running the place for them," his father answered.

"Mehy knows nothing about running a brewery. He is going to run it into the ground," the breweress said, her voice heavy with regret. This was a place that they had built with their sweat and blood, and the thought that it won't be cared for after they left, broke her heart.

The moment the mattresses were laid down and covered with linen sheets, the three younger ones, a boy and two girls began fighting for the softest bed for the night. The girls won the fight.

Their son was older and more mature - he wasn't interested in picking the best bed for himself, instead, he had questions.

"I know that we are selling the place because we've got a good deal and we also get to move to a better city. I understand that. But what flummoxes me is - why are *they* coming here?"

It was a question that both the brewer and the breweress had already struggled to answer.

"According to Mehy, they grew up in Philae. Their parents worked on the construction of the temple. Now they've made their money in the delta and they want to return, maybe to live out their old age here," she explained.

Anyway, it didn't matter. In a few weeks they would be in Memphis, starting a new life.

ᴡᴡ ﻼﻼ ᴡᴡ

When the brewer's family was bidding farewell to the city they had spent most of their life in, a nondescript galley was sailing up the Nile.

It was a trader's galley. Among the galleys, the boats,

and the skiffs going up and down the Nile, it did not stand out, which was excellent, for it carried a precious cargo. The purpose for which this trader's galley was headed south, was hidden in a secret room within its hull, and even those who worked the oars or cleaned the vessel did not know what it was.

The old trader who was the captain of this galley, however knew everything, and for his knowledge he was so revered that everyone called him *Iry-pat,* or the noble father. He knew about the charge he was carrying and he knew who would profit from his venture and when. He knew that he too would profit, and yet, in his mind raged a storm so strong that it allowed him no respite at all. While his charge was comfortable in the belly of his vessel, he stood upon the deck, sweating for no apparent reason at all.

The nearest ship that he could see on the northern horizon was closing in, slowly but surely. The ship could belong to anyone. It could belong to Mark Antony who was an ally of his charge, or to Octavian, the new Caesar of Rome. He scanned the length of Nile once again. The galleys in between were many, and they all looked the same, so unless the raiding ship knew exactly which ship or boat they were looking for, he and his charge would be safe.

Suddenly, the galley lurched. It did sometimes, when it was quickly steered to create a safe space between two vessels, or when the wind changed direction abruptly. The Captain cringed. His charge was of a volatile disposition, and the last thing that *Iry-pat* wanted was that he burst out of his hiding in plain view of the rowers.

His charge's was a face that Egypt knew too well.

He rushed down the deck, almost stumbling and falling over his toga. Togas, even the linen ones, were terribly uncomfortable in this hot weather, but a man of his status was expected to wear one.

He dashed down the steps and flung the curtains aside.

Inside was a small antechamber with wooden walls and rug-covered timber floor. Two stools and a short table were nailed to the floor. Right across, there was another door. He strode to it, carefully, and pushed the curtain aside. Inside, a young man of seventeen lounged upon a bed. Two women sat at his feet, massaging them, while he was sampling figs from a silver tray perched upon the table at the side of his bed.

"Your Highness, you must prepare yourself. I've noticed at least two naval ships behind us and they are closing in. They will be upon us before morning," he bowed to drop a quick curtsey.

The boy turned to look at him. *Iry-pat* noticed that he had neither his father's temperament nor looks. In his youth, Julius Caesar must have been wiry man with small eyes and a big nose. Caesarion here was reasonably handsome with a dense thatch of reddish hair. He had big eyes that were widely spaced on his attractive face.

If Caesarion were saved, could he be a better ruler than Cleopatra? Iry-pat wondered and involuntarily shook his head.

"The military ships…they could be Uncle Antony's," Caesarion mused, disengaging his feet from the attention of the women and standing up.

Iry-pat had thought the same, but the likelihood of their nautical pursuers belonging to Caesarion's Uncle Antony was exceedingly small, almost non-existent. When they had left Alexandria, he had heard the rumors.

"What do *you* think, *Iry-pat?*" Caesarion persisted.

Persistence among the young brats was another reason why *Iry-pat* abhorred this mission. When Cleopatra had called him and given him the responsibility of carefully ferrying the future Pharaoh of Egypt to the eastern shores and putting him on a ship to India, he had willingly agreed. It was true that he didn't have the option of refusing the Pharaoh of Egypt, but he had later wondered whether his mission had been burdened with misfortune right from the beginning. He knew the risks that he would run, but he had failed to mention them to Cleopatra. He knew why.

Her bewitching eyes had enthralled him.

But how could he be blamed for it. When two Great Roman Generals Julius Caesar and Mark Antony could be completely swept off their feet by Cleopatra's charisma, *Iry-pat* was just an official in her court.

"*Iry-pat?*"

He heard anger in Caesarion's voice. The fruit of the future Pharaoh's anger might be delayed, but *Iry-pat* will have to eat it sooner or later.

"Your Highness," he replied tentatively, trying not to promise too much, "it's not possible to say. They are still far away. But it will not hurt to be prepared. When you hear my whistle, disguise yourself into your priest's robes and go into the alley. Reach the escape-hatch and open it. You will find a boat lowered and waiting to ferry you ahead."

Caesarion laughed. His young white teeth sparkled, making *Iry-pat* think how callow his ward was. But Cleopatra too was eighteen when she had become Pharaoh. He thought and swallowed his feeling of unease. Perhaps when the double crown settled upon his brow, he would mature. In the previous year, Cleopatra had announced Caesarion as the co-ruler of Egypt. So far, he had been a co-ruler only in name, for Caesarion had never been called upon to make decisions – and he still had the attitude of a brat.

"Your Highness," he plodded on. "You must remember the protocol. When you leave the galley, be sure that no proof of your identity remains on your person."

Caesarion quirked a brow, and made *Iry-pat* wonder if his ward had understood anything at all. Whether his mother's cold blood coursed in his veins or not, would soon be clear. *Iry-pat* feared that the boy was very different from his mother.

Plunging his sword into the hearts of the two women with whom he had journeyed this far, wouldn't be an easy call for young Caesarion.

He curtsied again and withdrew from the royal presence. Behind him trailed a string of murmurs and giggles. He shook his head in dismay.

Egypt was no more the land of gods and pharaohs. The last three hundred years had changed it into a vassal state of other lesser nations, and now, he, *Iry-pat*, a true-blood Egyptian had stopped believing that things could go back to being the way they were.

Outside, on the breast of the Nile, another trade galley crossed them. It was going downstream, perhaps to the delta. On the deck stood a gaggle of children that waved at *Iry-pat*, reminding him of his own family that he had left behind in Memphis.

᚜ ᚜᚜᚜ ᚜

Cleopatra swept up the marble steps and across the mosaic of lotus blooms that bordered the cool marble floor. Her own chambers were the most luxurious ones in the whole palace. The palace was a strange combination of Greco-Egyptian architecture, but the entire décor was Egyptian. The etched and painted pillars, the covered limestone walls, even the high roofs – they all gave the place a majestic feel.

Oblivious of the splendor around her, Cleopatra tore into her antechamber. Menas the eunuch and the girls remained outside. Apollo sat upon a low stool in the corner of the room, next to the cornice that carried a bust of Cleopatra's father Ptolemy the twelfth.

Apollo looked tired. His hair disheveled. Absently she

noted that he too was beginning to show the signs of age. His dark Sicilian hair was thinning at the top and his gaunt face was etched with the lines both fine and strong. Time and life had ravaged his body and her soul – perhaps his soul too, but he never bared it to Cleopatra so that she could see his wounds.

He looked tired but the moment she entered, he rose from his seat and curtsied. She motioned him to sit down.

"Is it done?" she asked. There was no time for trivialities. No point in asking how his journey had been and whether Nile was already beginning to turn turgid to signal the impending inundation. They were on a mission, and it was important that everything was done right and on time.

Apollo nodded.

Cleopatra had sat down upon a couch adjacent to his stool and pulled her legs up. Apollo averted his eyes, but a shadow of desire crossed his face.

"When will the vats arrive?" she asked.

"In ten days from now, they will be delivered at your mausoleum," he replied. Then he added, "Are you sure that you want to go ahead with it?"

She considered his question. A thin, bitter smile spread upon her face.

"What?" Apollo read her expression and enquired.

"There is no other way. I'll be meeting him tonight, but my heart tells me that *Shayt* had other plans for me. I am almost forty and he is barely thirty-three, and I have been his uncle's wife."

Apollo chuckled and countered her.

"That doesn't matter. It should not. It isn't as if you were his own father's wife."

Cleopatra smiled wryly. It was odd. The way the Romans were hung up about relationships. When her ancestor, Ptolemy the Second, had married his sister Arisnoe, they had called him Ptolemy *Philadelphus*, or the sibling-*loving* Ptolemy. Cleopatra had married two of her own brothers but she was sure that there was no love there. Nobody could ever accuse her of loving any of her siblings, even platonically.

"I must try. He hates me, I know. He hopes to parade me in his Triumph, I know that too. *Shayt* has helped me repair my torn fate twice before. When I had gone to Caesar and then to Antony, on both occasions I had felt her shadow walk by my side. I am not sure if *Shayt* would be there for me tonight," she pondered.

Apollo stood up and placed his hand upon her shoulder.

"Your Majesty, we must not lose hope. I will be there outside the door, and the shadow of the goddess *Shayt* would be inside with you. Neither of us would abandon you ever."

She looked up into the eyes of her childhood friend and her most trusted lieutenant. Hope surged in her heart.

"I am tired of these games, Apollo," she confessed. "But I must play them, for I was born a Ptolemy. I must do it for my family and for Egypt."

There was a knock at the door.

"It's Menas," she said, "I must prepare myself to meet Caesar's nephew and the new Emperor of the Roman Empire. It amuses me to think of that awkward, gangling nephew of Caesar as an emperor, and yet, if I must seduce him, I can't meet him looking like an old hag, can I?"

Apollo stood up, his eyes riveted to hers.

"Just talk. Talk to him in your own way - with your eyes. Your Majesty, with your words, you can bring the world to your feet."

She stood up on her toes and planted a kiss on his cheek.

"Thank you," she whispered, closing her eyes. She felt him leave through the movement of air that rushed in to fill the space he vacated.

It was time that she got ready.

"Charmion! Iras!" she called her handmaidens. The girls rushed in. They had been with her for many long years – they were more her family than her brothers and her sister were. She loved them as much as she loved her siblings, but she trusted them more. In her world, trust mattered more than love.

Cleopatra and her handmaidens then entered her bed-chamber. Inside her armoire were her dresses – classified by the purpose for which she wore them. Tonight she needed to wear a dress from the drawers at the left. The left-side drawers had remained untouched for many long years and she wasn't sure if she would be able to fit herself in many of them. The dress that she wanted to wear tonight was a gown of deep red silk that had a mesh of gold for a bustier. She would wear her gold crown with the wings of *Nekhbeth* the vulture goddess protecting her ears, and the hood of *Uraeus* the cobra protecting her forehead.

The two women pulled the drawer out. They removed the dress carefully and placed it upon the bed. Attached to the bedroom was another room, bigger in size, with a pool in the center. The pool was now filled with warm water fragrant with lilies. The room had a high roof supported by four extra columns that had scenes painted from her life in Rome. The walls had tall windows that ran up almost to the ceiling. Upon the windowsills stood pots with vines growing in them. This was Cleopatra's bath, and possibly the most luxurious room in the whole palace.

Cleopatra shrugged out of her linen gown and carefully stepped into her marble bathing pool. The soft warmth of the water tickled her feet. She felt the water touch her skin, wetting it as she slowly sank in it, until only her head was above the surface.

As she lay there with Charmion and Iras lathering her body, her thoughts grew wings and flew into the past.

She remembered the time when she was young, no more than eighteen. Her brothers were too young to help their father – too young and too foolish, and so Ptolemy the Twelfth, or Pharaoh Auletes, as he was affectionately called for he loved playing the pipe, had chosen his brilliant and perceptive daughter to assist him.

Those were the days when she was the happiest. It was the time when the beast of ambition had not yet trampled upon the innocence of her youth, and when she hadn't learned that death was an instrument of political strategy.

Then her father had died, and to complicate matters, he had left behind a will. Had he not left the will, a lot of things would have happened differently. But he had, and today, she found difficulty in remembering her father with the fondness that she once felt for him.

The will, the wretched will, spelled out that Egypt would be co-ruled by Cleopatra and her ten-year-old brother Theos, or Ptolemy the thirteenth or Philopater Ptolemy, and to ensure the purity of the bloodline, they would have to marry…each other.

Philopater Ptolemy?

Philopater Cleopatra?

Philopater meant father loving. It might have been true once, when she was a child, but as a grown woman she had learned about her father's follies, and she no longer loved him as she once did.

Philopater, she was not. Not anymore.

She must have chuckled, for her handmaidens had momentarily stopped lathering her body. They were her closest confidantes, after Apollodorus of course, but physically a lot closer. She opened her thighs, allowing their hands to reach between them. Their hands were soft and loving and the water aided them in their quest. Then Iras moved behind her as Charmion's continued to work the lather between her thighs, softly rolling her fingers upon the point where her spirit met her physical form, while Iras massaged her shoulders, reaching lower, on the sides, and under her breasts, feeling their weight upon her hands. Cleopatra sighed and loosened her muscles, allowing their practiced hands to comfort her.

Her thoughts wandered off again.

Her brother Theos was an idiot. At first, she had accepted her fate and done what was expected of her. She had married him, and *co-ruled*. Actually, *she* had ruled. She had taken every decision, even the smallest one, on behalf of her brother, calling him only to put his seal on the decisions. There were many who called him a puppet-head, and many more who saw an opportunity in the situation.

She hadn't lost her innocence until then. She hadn't seen the evil that was lurking behind her brother's eyes.

When Theos had turned twelve, he had demanded consummation of their marriage. It had horrified her, even though she had expected it to happen, sooner or later. But she hadn't expected her refusal to turn him so vituperative. He had stormed into her bedchamber one evening and found her with Apollo, and then he had raised a storm. He had called her names that she didn't quite see coming from her little brother. The next morning, in front of his small obsequious coterie, which included that dirty old conniving eunuch Ponthius who had aligned himself with her Theos, he had repudiated her.

He had repudiated her. The young whippersnapper had disowned her because she had, presumably, dishonored her husband.

She had got the whole episode obliterated from the scrolls of the royal scribes since, but the memory of it still rankled.

Suddenly she found the bath no longer comforting, and the soft hands of her handmaidens felt like snakes slithering upon her body. She didn't want anymore to do with the snakes – not now, not before she went to meet Octavian.

She jerked out of the water, splashing it about and throwing the women off-balance.

"Enough!" she ordered, "help me out."

They helped her out of the bath and then with a thick

absorbent towel made of many soft layers of linen, they began drying her body.

Charmion was the older of the two, and she had been more than just a handmaiden to Cleopatra. She had been her advisor and a friend so loyal that she wouldn't think twice before laying her life down for her mistress. Iras competed with her older counterpart in loyalty, but not in intelligence and cunning. And yet, Iras had a skill that made her almost indispensable. She was an incredible masseuse who could squeeze out every bit of tiredness from Cleopatra's body. She needed them both to be around her, all the time.

As they draped the red silk around her, gathering the pleats in the right places using the gold belt that she had procured in Rome, she considered the mammoth task that lay in front of her.

She needed to seduce the new Caesar with her will, wile, or wealth.

He would succumb to one of these. Of this she was sure – *well, almost.*

〰〰 ⟨⟨⟨ 〰〰

On the quiet and peaceful Nile, the galley that carried the future of Egypt in its womb continued to move south. The rowers rowed against the current, and the sounds the oars made broke the silence with a regular rhythm, lulling its passengers into a false sense of security.

The future Pharaoh of Egypt was, however, far from asleep. The women wouldn't let him sleep. Stuck in this tiny room, hidden from the world, he was getting restless. He hadn't seen the open sky, the reed-clad shores, or even the water of the Nile since he boarded this grotesque pile of wood. He remembered how horrible the boat looked on the outside. A blue and white *wadjet* eye painted on either side was the only ornament it had. The *wadjet* eye or the eye of Horus was painted on every other boat to ward off evil. It was so common that it had rendered the galley inconspicuous, the right opposite of the kind of vessel a king must travel in. But that, *Iry-pat* had told him, was the very reason why this galley had been chosen to ferry him.

All this, he had made peace with, but the worst of it all was that the chamber-pot was right there, in this tiny room with not more than a cubit to spare on all sides of the bed, and when he used it, the women were still there. They faced the opposite wall to give him his privacy, but he felt conscious of the sounds and smells that escaped his nether region when he sat upon that pot. It made him feel terrible for a few hours, but when evening fell, he forgot it all. In the dim light of the oil lamps, even his small prison looked inviting.

He had himself chosen the two women to accompany him on this journey. His mother had asked him to take along two servants who he could trust with his life. Obviously, she had no idea how intolerably boring his journey would be if he had followed her advice. He knew he would be safe in any case. Whatever his mother might say, he had never been in any real danger before. So he had chosen his favorites from his harem. The Egyptian and the Celt. The Egyptian was about fifteen years older than he was, but she made him feel like he ruled the world. The Celt was fresh and young, a year or two younger than him, and the Egyptian was tutoring her well. He loved the color of her skin, her beautiful blue eyes, and her hair that was spun from gold.

He knew them well, and he was confident that they knew their purpose in life. They existed for him – to please and entertain him.

This was why he was right now poised upon the Egyptian love-goddess, whose soft and fleshy thighs were open on either side of him, inviting him inside, while the Celt behind him was intent upon his jewels, her luscious lips and teasing tongue exciting him further, hardening and strengthening his purpose.

All Grecian, he himself was of a deep olive complexion, lighter than the Egyptian below him, and darker than the Celt behind.

The Egyptian seductress had learned her craft over many years, and had a new trick for him every night. Tonight she lay there sucking her thumb and pleasuring herself with her other hand. The woman's machinations made his passion burgeon, making him blind to everything except his destination. The two pylons guarding the entrance were shaking rhythmically as the woman's dancing fingers showed him the way.

He thrust himself in and made her squeal. The sound spurred him on. Enslaved by his stele upon which his whole existence now centered, he entered the soft and inviting cave. Once inside, his monster, still incited to continue its rampage by the Celt's soft mouth, ravaged and plundered. Moans, groans, and shrieks of pleasure filled the air, drowning out the sound of the whistle blown outside on the deck.

When Octavian's men tore open the trapdoor and trundled down, they found the co-regent of Egypt pummeling himself into the matron below and the young Celt attempting to keep herself attached to his bottom, her golden hair bouncing upon her shoulders.

ᴡᴡᴡ 𓏲𓏲𓏲 ᴡᴡᴡ

Cleopatra alighted from the palanquin at the main entrance of the guest wing of the palace. Charmion and Iras followed her as she ascended the steps. In the last twenty years, this was her second visit to this wing. The first had been when her brother had made that colossal error of having Pompei killed.

She remembered it all in vivid detail.

She was in exile when the Roman General Pompei who had been defeated by his political rival Julius Caesar, had sought asylum in Egypt. Her brother and husband Theos had exiled her on the advice of that cunning sycophant, the eunuch Ponthius. Ponthius, the scheming scum, had advised Theos that since between the two, Caesar was more powerful than Pompei, Egypt must align itself to Julius Caesar, and that Caesar would be pleased if his rival Pompei was eliminated.

Theos had followed the advice of Ponthius, and Pompei was beheaded upon his arrival on the shores of Egypt. When Caesar, in his pursuit of Pompei, had arrived in Alexandria, Theos had presented Pompei's head to Caesar hoping that Caesar would be pleased.

The fool!

She had known even then how it would all play out, and so she had planned her own meeting with Caesar. It had to be done surreptitiously, if it were to succeed, and getting herself delivered inside a roll of carpet was an idea that she still remembered fondly as one of her best ones.

As she swept across the magnificent hall, to her left was the room where she had once met and seduced Caesar. She ignored the sharp pang in her heart as she glanced at it, and walked on. Octavian had set up his quarters in a suite of rooms that were meant to receive the kings and the queens of other countries. She remembered seeing him as a boy of fifteen, and wondered how he must have changed in all these years.

She didn't have to wait long. Octavian was there, in the antechamber, waiting for her. It pinched her heart to see the laurel wreath upon his brow. She had seen it so often, touched it, felt it, and even kissed it when it had graced the head of Julius Caesar.

But now Octavian was the new Caesar. Augustus Caesar. And the wreath now belonged to him.

He stood slightly taller than Julius. When Cleopatra entered, he bowed and curtsied. She still was the Queen of Egypt and he was the supreme commander of the Roman military.

The surprise in his eyes told her that she had momentarily dazzled him. It was a strong beginning and she found her confidence bolstered.

"Octavian," she began, "I suppose we must start with a cup of wine."

His eyes narrowed, but he complied and poured wine into two cups. She glanced at the label on the pitcher. It was a three-times good wine, which meant that it was more than a hundred years old.

Octavian had already started raiding the treasures of Egypt.

She took the silver cup from him, letting her fingers brush against his hand.

Octavian softly held her elbow and steered her to the couches. The couches were still covered in silk and the carpets under their feet were soft. She sat down and pulled her legs up. She knew that the posture added to her allure by exaggerating her curves.

"What was it that you wanted to talk about?" she asked, her voice low and mellifluous.

Octavian looked at her, his eyes stopping only for a moment upon her face then sliding down to her bare shoulders, and slipping into her cleavage. But he checked himself and his eyes returned to his cup.

Cleopatra saw it all and understood. She leaned back and placed her elbow upon the cushion, pushing her chest out. The red pleats of her gown camouflaged her aging body quite well. She had little doubt that she could pull it off.

Octavian watched her, his large eyes going where she wanted them to go.

"Tell me, Caesar. What would you have me do?" she looked at him askance, daring him to let his defenses drop.

Octavian rose and walked to the table to pick up a scroll.

"Here," he said, pushing the scroll into her hand, "here you'll find what I want."

She went through the list. It was a long one. It asked her for everything. Her crown, her palace, her mausoleum, and her fabled wealth! The room swam before her eyes. Octavian wasn't here to trade. *What would Cleopatra get in turn, if she gave it all away to him?*

"You want everything?" she asked haltingly.

"Only if you force me to ask for everything. I don't want to and I will not, if you don't force me," he explained.

"Are you threatening me?" she questioned him, her voice turning stern and losing its cloak of seduction.

Octavian didn't answer her. Instead he moved closer, until his face was barely a palm length away from hers. She could smell the Greek in him – the smell of leather and bronze, and she felt a chill creep up the nape of her neck.

"Are you attempting to seduce me?" he asked her back.

She held his gaze, unwavering and confident. He moved back a few paces.

"I am trying to strike a deal with you," he measured his words as he spoke, "I'll let you keep everything that is listed on that scroll, and I'll protect your interests. But I want something from you."

Cleopatra felt the chill pour down her spine making her heartbeats go up up and turning her hands clammy. Her dignified exterior began melting away as she put her feet down and sat erect with her hands in her lap.

"If what they say about you is true, what you want might be impossible to give," she said haltingly for her breath was caught in her throat.

"Give me Caesarion," he replied, turning his back to her.

He cannot look into my eyes. There still is hope, she thought.

Cleopatra laughed. She knew her laughter must've sounded raucous, even shrill, but at this moment she didn't care.

"You will never find him," she said, chewing every word then spitting it on him.

Octavian turned to face her. His eyes had now grown icy cold.

"He will be found. Trust me. And when he is, I will not arrest him, nor exile him, I will kill him. And then everyone will suffer. You have other children. I am not sure how much you care for them, or even for Antony, but I know of one person who you truly care about," he paused.

She looked at him, her brows lifted in curiosity.

"You. I know that you love yourself the best. I'll take you back to Rome where I will parade you in my Triumph, and I promise you a fate worse than you had inflicted upon Arisnoe. Think about it, Cleopatra. You killed your brothers in cold blood. What difference would a dead son make? You'll forget him and rule Egypt. Think about it."

Cleopatra listened to him carefully.

His threat to parade her in his Triumph made her anxious. When the Roman Generals returned after raiding other countries, their arrival in Rome was celebrated as a gala event, which was known as the Triumph. The returning heroes rode through the streets of Rome with music playing and drums beating, parading their spoils of war. She had maneuvered Mark Antony into displaying her own sister Arisnoe in his Triumph – a revenge that she had exacted from Arisnoe for joining her brothers and revolting against her. She would never let it happen to her, even if it meant the death of Cleopatra.

Men, she knew, loved the sound of their own voice, and she wouldn't stop him from listening to his. When he stopped, Cleopatra turned to leave, but before leaving, she whispered a single word.

"Never."

Octavian heard her.

"Never?" he laughed. "Don't sleep tonight. Spend the night ruminating, Cleopatra. You came here hoping to seduce me. Just the way you had seduced my uncle and adopted father Julius Caesar – but you were then about twenty and Uncle Julius had forgotten what it felt like to be fawned upon by an intelligent young woman. You thought that like Mark Antony, I'd be blinded by your glitz and glamor and not see you for what you are. But I do, Cleopatra, I see exactly what you are. Middling and wrinkling, bitter and spent, and yet you are in many ways quite like the vulture that sits upon your brow, rapacious and greedy, waiting to feed upon the carrion of Egypt. Your heart doesn't beat, for it is made of stone. Your afterlife for which you have been collecting things all your life, would end as soon as your green god *Anubis* weighs your heart, for it would be heavier than the steles of granite that you and your ancestors have raised along the Nile, and then that pathetic creature of the underworld…what is it called?" he stopped, searching for the name.

"*Ammit*," she supplied the name in a hoarse whisper.

"Yes, *Ammit* would shred your heart to pieces and eat it with relish," Octavian completed his thought.

Cleopatra didn't reply. She hadn't expected this deluge of hatred from him.

"You hate me," she observed.

Octavian took a deep breath and forced a smile.

"Go back, Cleopatra, and reflect upon your misdeeds. Your hunger for the crown has brought you to this. I am asking you to sacrifice just one more life on the altar of Cleopatra's ambitions, and you get to keep the double crown for as long as you are alive."

Cleopatra listened as she watched her reflection upon the shiny surface of the wine flask. She could say a lot of things, but knew that it was wiser to stay silent.

"Do you accept it?" Octavian asked her.

She heard the pitch of his voice change, and sensed danger.

It was time to flee.

᠕᠕ ۩۩ ᠕᠕

Antony,

King of my heart, ruler of my ka,

You know that I've loved you always. I spent eleven years in your embrace, loving you, bearing your children, hoping that one day, peace would descend upon Egypt. Hoping that you and I together will be able to establish a kingdom that would prosper beyond our lives.

But this is not to be. Antony, my heart is now broken, because I know now that evil has come to Egypt. It has come here in the person of Octavian. First he won the war and we lost it, then he established himself in Alexandria and we slept – now, he intends to kill us all – in body and spirit.

I know that the body doesn't matter. It's a vessel for the ka and the ba. But spirit matters, and he intends to break my spirit by displaying me in his Triumph.

I don't fear death, for it is only a step toward afterlife. I fear being paraded as a trophy of war. I fear watching you die. I fear watching my children die. To overcome my fears, I must die. I hope the children are safe. I know that Caesarion is, but for how long, I do not know, for Octavian is determined to murder him.

As long as Caesarion lives, Octavian will always be afraid of an uprising; he would worry that Romans might rally behind Caesarion for they loved his father Julius. I cannot give up Caesarion for he is my son, my co-ruler and the future Pharaoh of Egypt, and Caesarion's life is the only payment that Octavian would accept in lieu of letting me keep the crown. You and I, both know that even then, I shall be the Queen only in name.

And so, my heart's hope and desire, when this missive reaches you,

I will be no more. I'll die here, in my mausoleum, and I will take along the treasures of Egypt, so that Octavian may never lay his evil eyes upon them. I will sleep upon my bed in my mausoleum, so that he doesn't insult my death by not burying me with my treasures, as a pharaoh should be.

With this missive, I write the final story of my life.

We will meet again in the afterlife.

In your love, with your dreams forever,

*   - Cleopatra*

The missive that was meant for Mark Antony was intercepted by Octavian's men and taken to him.

For almost a week now, Cleopatra had shut herself inside her mausoleum, with her two handmaidens. The doors of the mausoleum opened only twice – in morning and evening. The handmaidens admitted those who brought in the supplies for Pharaoh's burial, and then shut the door again. Today Charmion had approached one of the guards and handed him the message for Antony.

The guards had instructions to deliver all the communication that emerged from the mausoleum to Octavian's office, and so the scroll was now lying open in front of him.

He scratched his chin as he paced up and down, his toga swishing with the violence of his step.

Then, coming to a decision, he stopped abruptly, and harked for the guard.

"Take this letter to Antony immediately. Tell him that Cleopatra sent you to deliver it."

The guard took the scroll, confirmed his understanding of the instruction, and left. Antony's camp was set up not half a league away. He would deliver the missive to Antony within an hour.

Octavian dropped himself into the couch that Cleopatra had sat upon the other day. He wondered what made the woman so alluring. She was a Grecian with not even a drop of Egyptian blood in her, but by the Greek standards of beauty, her face would be considered average. And now, she wasn't even young. Yet, when he closed his eyes and replayed their meeting over, he felt himself being drawn to her.

Since that afternoon meeting with Cleopatra, he had been thinking if he blamed his uncle anymore. She had gone to him, a young woman, her face innocent, her body callow, and her mind devious. She must have been irresistible. Even now, she was difficult to resist, and if succumbing to her ways had not been a political suicide, he would have allowed her to add him to his list of conquests.

Why?

The question was impossible to answer.

Because of her bewitching eyes?

Because she had a voice that addressed a man's libido?

Because she dressed up to conjure a picture of Venus herself?

His thoughts were muddied, and no clear answer emerged.

It was the commotion outside that brought him back to reality. Outside, he heard the guards talking in rushed loud voices.

"Come in," he bellowed, and a guard stumbled in. He was the same man he had sent to deliver the message.

"Caesar, there's terrible news," he said, still out of breath. "I had delivered the message and was about to leave, when I learned that after reading the letter General Antony had tried to kill himself by falling upon his sword."

Octavian's light brown eyes narrowed.

"Is he dead?" he asked.

᭟᭟᭟ ꠸꠸꠸ ᭟᭟᭟

At the mausoleum, the vats were being downloaded.

They were huge vats of fine wine matured for more than a hundred years. Cleopatra didn't touch any wine that wasn't at least a hundred years old and she wasn't going to change in her afterlife.

Actually, Cleopatra wasn't even sure if she would ever get past the gatekeepers of *Duat*. Octavian was right when he spoke of her heart being heavy with the guilt of her brother's murders, and so even if there were an afterlife, she wouldn't make it past the heart-eating monster *Ammit*.

She stood in the antechamber, inspecting the vats that contained the wine. They were smaller than the beer vats but that was fine. They were there only for camouflage.

The beer vats, however, were a different matter.

They were the right size, but the one that she was waiting for hadn't arrived yet.

She knew that Apollo would have done his best – if not inspired by his loyalty to her then motivated by his love for his own life, for his life was on the line too.

Yet, she would have been at peace if things had moved at the right pace. Everything was lined up, the way they had planned. For many nights she had not been able to sleep without filling her room with the smoke of cannabis, and this morning, she had even taken the final step by writing to Antony.

Now there was no going back.

And then there was also the matter of sealing the entrance, which couldn't be done until…the right vat arrived.

"It's here," Iras announced. She was slightly out of breath. She too hadn't been sleeping well, and while Charmion knew everything about the plan, Iras was told only what she needed to know. Cleopatra had planned everything down to the minutest detail.

She knew well that any political strategy could fall flat without a detailed tactical plan, and even the best of plans could be ruined if they weren't executed correctly. She understood it better than her predecessors – perhaps better than anyone else.

The way she had planned and executed her first meeting with Antony, was as close to perfect as anyone could get. Eleven years ago, when she had received Antony's summons, she had bristled. She was a Queen, and he was a mere General – an officer who served Rome. But then she had thought it over and realized that there was no other way for her to keep her kingdom, than to heed Antony's call.

So she had sailed on a barge lying upon its poop deck, which she had got covered with a thin leaf of gold. She still remembered it all in detail, for she had designed every bit of that experience that historians and poets will write about. The rich purple sails of her barge, she was sure, must have been seen by Antony's cronies long before the barge had reached the city of Tarus. The pavilion under which she lay was made of gold-sheets, and she herself was dressed to look like Venus. Little boys with wings strapped upon their shoulders, imitated Cupid. They held little fans, which they waved to keep her cool. Incenses and fragrances rode upon the cool breeze that blew from the barge to the banks of river Cydnus. She had taken along musicians with lutes and flutes and singers who sang the songs of love. A dozen lovely women either danced or frolicked to complete the Greek vision of heaven, while Cleopatra's ethereal presence presided over the whole display.

Poor Antony. He had no choice, she thought. A smile crept up the corners of her lips.

She had spent eleven years with Antony, and bore him three children. He loved her, she knew, and through his love for her, he had indebted her to him. Today, through her missive, she had paid her debt. It would free Antony. Octavian only wished to harm Antony because Antony loved her. The least she could do for the man who had loved her all these years, was to send him safely back to his wife.

Even she, Cleopatra the heartless, could do this.

It was time that they all went their own separate ways.

"Your Majesty, it's here," Iras repeated.

"Ask them to bring it in," Cleopatra instructed Iras, slightly incensed at the girl's insistence.

The vat was rolled in. It looked exactly like the other vats that were already there.

The men who had brought the vat in, left soon after their task was done.

Nobody would guess a thing.

"We must check," said Charmion, but Cleopatra shook her head.

"Why not?" Charmion asked, perplexed.

"Not now. I trust Apollo's word."

Charmion wasn't convinced, but she couldn't counter the Queen, so she acquiesced and returned to the side of Cleopatra.

"Your Majesty, should I draw you a bath?" Iras asked politely.

Cleopatra thought it over for a moment then nodded. She needed some time alone with Charmion. After Iras had left, she turned to Charmion.

"Do you think that my missive reached him?" she asked.

The missive, Charmion had earlier pointed out to Cleopatra, wasn't one of her brighter ideas. She was sure that the missive must have found its way to Octavian. Whether it reached Antony or not was of smaller consequence than the fact that it might have landed in Octavian's grasping hands.

"I don't know," Charmion replied truthfully, "but I still think that the General would have been able to handle it on his own. That missive could prove dangerous for you."

Cleopatra shook her head vigorously.

"Charmion," she said, "I must bring Octavian's attention on me. My death would be a spectacle that would have the attention of both Rome and Egypt. When everyone would be watching Alexandria and talking about me, Caesarion would have the opportunity to slip away unnoticed."

"Octavian might have found him already," whispered Charmion.

"He hasn't, or he would have mentioned it. Why would he not use that information to threaten me, if he had Caesarion?" Cleopatra asked, her knit brows belying her words.

Charmion looked at her mistress. Cleopatra appeared now to be but a shadow of her former self. She stood there in midst of the beer vats that were almost as tall as her, wearing a simple gown of white linen, her breasts sagging in the fold of her gown over her belt. She wore little make up today, only her eyes were lined in black, and upon her head, she wore no wig, allowing her real hair to be seen. She had begun to henna her hair a few years ago, and the red streaks shone under the yellow lights of the lamps. Under the kind glow of the lamps, her wrinkles couldn't be seen, but Charmion knew where each was. She knew her mistress's face better than her own.

Charmion remembered that she hadn't answered Cleopatra's question. *Why Octavian wouldn't tell Cleopatra, if he had indeed captured Caesarion?*

"He may not have mentioned it because he is waiting for an opportune time, or, you may be right. He might not have reached Caesarion," she acknowledged.

"For Egypt's sake, I hope that he hasn't. Caesarion is the last of the Ptolemies, and the last of Caesar," Cleopatra said.

It was when Iras stumbled in, her face white and her breath short, that they realized that something was amiss. The faded sounds that floated in were coming from the street outside.

"Your Highness," Iras burbled, "It's the General."

"What about the General?" Cleopatra rushed to the distraught girl and shook her shoulders.

"He is wounded. They have him on a stretcher under the window of your bedchamber and they are saying that he has tried to kill himself. They want to bring him in. Should I open the entrance?" Iras continued to gabble incoherently.

Cleopatra clambered out to the entrance with Iras and Charmion in her wake. A myriad questions swirled in her mind.

Did she incite Antony to commit suicide by sending him that letter? How could she not have anticipated this – she knew that Antony loved her beyond reason, didn't she?

"Your Highness," Charmion called from behind, but Cleopatra ignored her. Instead she directed Iras to open the entrance. Charmion hurled herself in Cleopatra's path and opened her arms to block her way.

"Your Highness, listen to me. We don't know if the men who've borne him here belong to Octavian. Octavian would do anything to make you leave the mausoleum. Don't let a quirk of fate destroy your plans."

Cleopatra looked stricken, but she stopped. Iras stopped too.

"Ask them to bring him up through the window," Cleopatra instructed Iras.

༔ ༔ ༔

He opened his eyes, but saw nothing.

It was dark.

But it was never dark when he woke up. This was certainly odd. He shook his head and a wave of pain shot through his temple. Instinctively, Caesarion tried to raise his hand to check his head, but he couldn't. His hands were bound behind his back.

Something wasn't right.

The girls?

He called their names.

They weren't there.

And he wasn't on the galley. The floor wasn't rolling at all.

Where was he?

"Where am I?" he screamed.

There was no answer.

But soon he saw light – a horizontal line of orange light glowed on the floor in front of him, and realization began to dawn. It started to make sense - slowly at first, and then it all sank in with a resounding thud. He was in a room and the door of the room was closed. Someone was outside, possibly a guard, because in the orange strip of flickering light, he could see the shadow of his feet.

He screamed again. His screams rebounded from the walls and returned. His nervousness increased and his hands turned clammy. He felt his bowels clench and cramp and then he found himself losing control of both his bowels and bladder.

The relief was sudden and welcome. For a few moments there he had forgotten his plight. But after the relief evaporated, fear once again rushed in to fill the void.

And he screamed again.

᭝᭝᭝ ʘʘʘ ᭝᭝᭝

Cleopatra waited in the other room while Charmion and Iras directed the men, and helped them pull Antony up through the window. Sitting alone, she thought of the eleven years that she had given to him, and he, to her. They had been happy together, and Antony had loved her more than anyone could ever love her. He had loved her the way she was – with her cunning and knowledge; and her temperament and tantrums. He could have been Caesar, but he gave it all up, including his life in Rome. And yet, she hadn't expected him to kill himself.

She sat upon a low stool, listening to the sounds that floated in from her bedchamber, feeling empty inside. All the years that they had been together, she had loved him equally, if not more.

And yet, she felt nothing.

Except that she found herself thinking about how she would be handling this last minute inconvenience.

She caught herself thinking about how Antony's death would affect her plans, and she hated herself for it.

Was she truly heartless? She must have felt something - grief, sorrow, at least some temporary despair.

But she didn't.

Why?

Was she so wrapped in herself, so selfish in pursuit of her goals, that she didn't stop to appreciate Antony's love for her? Perhaps she was, because when she had sent that missive to him, she hadn't anticipated that he would kill himself. She had wanted to free him. He wasn't in danger from Octavian – and he could have returned to retire.

Instead, he had killed himself.

Tried to, she corrected herself. He was still not dead.

Why did he have to come here?

The answer was simple. Impulse ruled the life of Mark Antony – it was impulse that made him fall upon his sword, then have himself brought here. And it was impulse that had made him fall in love with Cleopatra. The man didn't think logically.

Now what was she to do? She was his wife and the mother of his children, and she had to put up appearances. If he were still alive, she could at least help ease his passing by reminding him of her love and telling him that she would meet him in the afterlife.

"Majesty, he is here," Iras peeked in through the curtains.

Cleopatra stood up, her face transforming into a landscape of grief. She stumbled into her bedchamber where Antony lay across her bed, blood still flowing out of his wound, soaking the sheet red.

"Antony," she screamed. "Oh Antony, Antony! Why did you do this?" she cried out loud enough for her voice to carry into the street.

Cleopatra then climbed upon the bed and placed Antony's head upon her lap. Her tears splashed upon his face as she bent down to kiss him upon his lips that were contorted with pain. Then with her eyes closed she raised her head and began beating her chest.

"Shhh…" Antony attempted to console her.

"Why did you do it?" she asked through her cries.

"Because," he gurgled, his blood flowing out stronger with each word he said, "I can't live without you. Now I'll die in peace, because I am in your arms. I'll wait for you in the afterlife."

And then he died. Despite his pain, he had a smile on his face.

The next morning, they would send his body out. She would wash his wound and bathe his body herself. He had already left this world and gone to the afterlife. If afterlife did exist, it would be great to have such a loyal friend there. She was sure that they had parted friends.

〰〰 ◊◊◊ 〰〰

The breweress came out upon the deck with her daughters, where she joined her husband. Since they had embarked upon their journey to the delta, they had been sleeping in the hold with all others. At first there were about twenty passengers.

Some got down in Thebes, then some others in Abydos, Asyut, and Herakleopolis. Now only their family remained on the galley.

"Where are the boys?" she asked her husband.

"They were here just moments ago," he smiled at her. He felt blessed to be her husband. She had been a good wife and an excellent mother, and their brewing business had grown mostly due to her. While he was away during the four months of monsoon, when every young or middling Egyptian man was called to work on one or the other construction project for the government, she had kept the brewery functioning.

"Doesn't it feel great to be on a galley where you are the only ones traveling. It's like you are special – like you own the galley," she said, looking at her husband. She too was glad to have him as her partner. True he was older than her by a few years and that he wasn't very rich, but he was a man who cared for his family and loved to spend time with them.

They were blessed by Shayt, the goddess of fortune.

"We have enough to buy a small boat," her husband smiled. He always wanted a boat in which he could go fishing and occasionally, take his family out on the Nile.

"Isn't it time for the afternoon meal?" she said, shading her eyes and looking up. The sun was upon their heads now.

The passengers were served their meals in the hold and the boys were already there when their parents and sisters came down.

"We came down with Mehy," quipped the brewer's younger son.

After helping them with the sale of their brewery in Ombo, Mehy was accompanying them to Memphis. He had family there, and he had also offered to help them buy a new place for their business.

"They tell me that they are happy about your moving to Memphis," Mehy observed.

The brewer smiled at his children indulgently and

nodded.

Mehy opened the reed-basket and began handing out their meals to them. The brewer was deeply appreciative of Mehy's gesture of accompanying them to Memphis. It didn't surprise him much though, for Mehy belonged to the delta, and he would be meeting his own family there, before he returned to Ombo.

"Our last lunch on the galley," the brewer said and the children smiled happily. They were waiting to run on solid ground, with warm dirt under their feet – they were all looking to start a new life – full of happy surprises.

"Yes, your last lunch…on the galley," Mehy gave him a wry smile. He had a tear in the corner of his eye, which glinted when he turned, but nobody saw it. This was the final task that his client had set him. He was to receive a thousand *drachmas* for the whole deed – from buying the brewery, to dispatching the family of the previous brewer to the afterlife, to running the brewery until his client arrived in Ombo took over.

And yet, Mehy wouldn't have agreed to kill the family not even for five thousand drachmas or ten, had he not known who the client was. His client was not to be crossed.

Much later that night, the galley deposited Mehy in Khunum and then sailed on silently floating upon the deep calm waters of the Nile.

The next morning Mehy would take the first galley back to Ombo, where he would run the brewery, till his client arrived.

The galley carried on to Memphis, where it docked in the quay, and the last of the merchandise that it carried in its hold was downloaded and carted away for burial.

Only the brewer was still alive when Mehy had disembarked in Khunum. He had been trying to open the trapdoor, but it was latched on the outside, and his insides were in turmoil. He had been vomiting blood since he ate his lunch.

Shayt had turned her back on them.

ᴍᴡ ᑫᑫᑫ ᴍᴡ

They had opened the vat after all negotiations with Octavian had failed. Cleopatra had tried again. She had sent him messages, and he had replied. They had attempted to negotiate, but their discussion was deadlocked.

And yet, there was a promise that Octavian had made – one that she trusted him to keep. He would care for her other two sons and only daughter, and never harm them. She trusted him to do that.

His ceaseless efforts at convincing her to stay alive had a clear purpose. If she died, the treasures that were held in her mausoleum would be buried along with her, and Octavian needed to lay his hands upon her riches, for he had to pay his army. She knew that the war had limited Octavian's resources severely. He needed the treasure of Egypt to keep his military together, and she wasn't going to let him have any of it.

Cleopatra knew that the next morning, everything would have changed.

She looked inside the vat and smiled with satisfaction. She was going to die a death worthy of Cleopatra. A death that shall paint a scene that would be remembered forever - a scene that for posterity would inspire poetry and plays, a drama that shall play into people's imagination for centuries to come.

She turned and asked Charmion for the basket.

"It is already here," said Charmion as she pointed to the beautifully painted reed basket that stood proudly upon a lidded vat.

"And everything else?" Cleopatra asked, cryptically.

Charmion understood and nodded.

Cleopatra looked at Charmion, and for the first time in

her life wondered what made someone this loyal. While there was still time before she took the final test to prove her loyalty, Charmion had willingly agreed to do everything.

It was her willful acceptance of everything that troubled Cleopatra. What Charmion was willing to do for her, Cleopatra herself would never do for another man or woman – not even for her flesh and blood.

ᴧᴧᴧ ⵡⵡⵡ ᴧᴧᴧ

Inside the darkroom, Caesarion had stopped trying to make sense of his situation. He had lost track of time.

But he had learned something important, and his first learning had led him to surmise the second.

First, that he was a prisoner of Octavian himself, and second, that he was not leaving this room alive.

Octavian hadn't condescended to come over himself. Either he didn't care, or they were far away from Alexandria. Caesarion didn't care to find out.

All that his tortured mind could now think was whether his mother even knew where he was? More than that, did she even care? He knew his mother well. She was a self-sufficient, confident woman who had always wanted him to be brave and courageous, and intelligent and cunning. But he was none of these. His mother never cared either for weakness or for the weak.

He was weak.

The door burst open, and a man holding a torch walked in. The shock of the door opening unexpectedly sent his heart racing.

In the flickering ochre light of the torch, the dank room's dirty floor and patchy walls came alive. He noticed that the room was small – five paces either ways. He sat in a puddle of his own excreta.

Caesarion squinted to see the man's face, trying to recognize him, but he didn't know who he was.

"Where am I?" he asked him, his throat parched and his dried lips bleeding.

"Still in Egypt, and you will soon be going back to Alexandria," came the answer. The man thrust the mouth of a water-skin into his mouth. "Drink," he said.

Caesarion drank. His thoughts faded, as the water splashed down his throat, inundating his insides. Nothing had ever given him such pleasure – nothing had ever tasted so good.

He didn't care if they killed him. Afterlife was going to be blissful.

꙳ ᚹᚹᚹ ꙳

The new breweress Hera and her husband had taken over the brewery in Ombo just six months ago. Slipping into their new roles hadn't been easy – for this was a life very different from what they had led in the past.

Hera had just settled upon her *diwan* in the chamber at the back of her wine shop that evening when she heard the news. A customer who said that he had traveled from Alexandria was talking to another. She had learned to ignore the salubrious jokes and raucous laughter of the breweries customers, but that customer had spoken a name, that had made her sit upright.

Caesarion.

His utterance of the name had sent her heart racing.

What was he saying about Caesarion?

She had wanted to rush out and talk to the man, but she was a practical person who knew how unwise and how terribly risky it could be. So she had stayed in her chamber, but listened intently.

Caesarion was dead.

Her son was killed. Octavian Augustus Caesar, the new Emperor of the Roman empire, had killed her son!

Caesarion was killed for being the son of Julius Caesar. He had died because of the elaborate lie that Cleopatra had woven.

She slipped down from the *diwan* upon the floor, letting the news of Caesarion's death wash over her, filling every pore of her being with hatred for Octavian.

Octavian, that lying snake, may he develop wounds that fester forever and may maggots and scarabs feast upon his body in front of his own eyes! That mendacious scoundrel had Caesarion all the time. All the time he was negotiating with her, he had her son.

The child, her sweet boy, didn't want to go. She had insisted that he did.

She wondered whether there was any other way by which she could have kept Caesarion alive. Possibly none. Octavian would have killed Caesarion anyway.

Then a murky and unclean thought occurred to her.

Had she given her son up of her own volition, she would still be Pharaoh. A puppet-pharaoh dancing to the tunes of Rome, yet a pharaoh!

She had lost everything for nothing.

Her son Caesarion had died for nothing.

Oh, Cleopatra, why?

All that planning came to a naught, didn't it?

The vat, the scene, the escape – everything was planned to perfection.

The woman inside the beer vat was bound and gagged, and to stop her from rattling while being transported, Apollo had added some extra linen packing. She was barely conscious when they dragged her out and laid her upon the bed.

Cleopatra had stood there assessing the woman's appearance while the handmaidens changed her clothes. They removed her simple linen shift then struggled to get her into Cleopatra's finest white linen gown.

"Let us paint a scene that would be remembered forever," she mused watching them prepare the woman.

Cleopatra had looked upon the woman's face and seen her own. The experience had left her amazed and distraught at the same time, for in that unconscious woman's face, she saw a middling matron with a big nose and sagging cheeks. The woman's skin had already lost its suppleness, and the impression of the sack's weave upon her cheek was still there after having been removed from the vat, like a banner waved by old age.

She had watched Charmion and Iras slide her signature armlets formed as coiled snakes, upon the woman's arms. Next they had slipped her pectoral around her shoulders, clipping it behind her neck. They had tied her most cherished gold belt around the woman's waist, before starting to paint her face. They had been painting Cleopatra's own face for years now, and before they finished, she saw herself upon the bed. She lay supine in repose, her upper body propped up a little upon the pillows and the cushions.

After helping the barely conscious lookalike of Cleopatra consume a deadly mixture of hemlock, opium, and wolfsbane, Iras and Charmion both had their last meal. Only Iras didn't know that it was her last. She had died before Cleopatra left. She had helped Charmion bring Iras to the bed and position her at the feet of the royal lookalike.

Administering the poison to Iras first was Charmion's idea. She had expected Iras to baulk at the thought of committing suicide, and so she had wanted to be sure.

"We have done it for you, your Majesty," she had said to Cleopatra when they were arranging the bed. The reed snake-basket was the final touch. They arranged it to look like it had fallen from the bed after the snake had bitten its victim and sent her in convulsions.

"One last detail," said Cleopatra. "Get me one of my hair-pins."

Upon the naked left breast of her lookalike, she made two puncture-holes. They were impossible to miss.

Now the scene was set.

The Last Queen of Egypt had embraced the Uraeus, and in the protection of the snake deity, she had traveled to the afterworld. Her two loyal handmaidens had consumed poison to accompany her – just the way they did in the times of the first kings.

Cleopatra went to the door and looked at the whole scene from the viewpoint of its first viewers.

They had waited until Apollo had brought the cart to the entrance, and then Charmion had consumed her own dose.

When Charmion had opened the vial, something had clawed at Cleopatra's heart and conscience. It was true that they had planned it all together. And yet, as hard-hearted as she was, the thought of losing Charmion made Cleopatra sad. In that moment of weakness, she had asked Charmion to escape with her.

"It is impossible, Your Majesty. They must find us both or they would wonder if I had assassinated you. Then they shall come after me, and find you. My death will seal it all in place."

Cleopatra had stepped forward and hugged Charmion – her only friend, other than Apollodorius. Charmion dissolved into tears. They had stood there, two women who in their own ways, had changed the way history shall be written, until they heard the knock.

Charmion disengaged herself from Cleopatra's embrace and went to the little window on the side from where she could see outside.

"They are here," she whispered.

Cleopatra climbed inside the vat marked with the *wadjet* eye.

"I've lived for you, and I'm honored to die for you,"

Charmion said. She wanted her end to be as fitting as her life.

After placing the lid upon the vat and sealing it, Charmion had pattered to the door and opened it.

As the vat that bore her was carried outside, Cleopatra was overwhelmed with the feeling of having been through it all, before. It was almost like the carpet again, except that since then, her innocence had died many deaths – sometimes it was killed by others, at other times, it had been throttled to death by her own hands.

Once outside on the *verandah*, she felt the vat being turned sideways before it began rolling and trundling down the steps. She bit her lip and tried not to make a sound. The vat was safely loaded and the cart had already turned the corner when she heard Charmion scream.

Sitting huddled inside the vat, bumping against its walls as the cart lumbered and hobbled on the stone-paved streets, she remembered thinking about the scene that she had left behind. She could see exactly what Octavian and his men would see when they broke the entrance door down and entered.

Six months had passed since the morning she had climbed inside the vat, and yet, with this news that she had just received from the north, her biggest show had turned into a joke. For now, she was dead in the eyes of the world, and her only hope to win Egypt back, her son Caesarion too now lay dead. Octavian had executed him in full public view.

At least he would have a tomb - modest but sufficient to help him journey into afterlife.

He was her first child. A child born when she was still innocent, when she could still love. Yet, today, the tears that fell from her eyes lamented not his death but her only chance of returning to Alexandria and ruling Egypt once again. She recognized it, and despised herself for it. This was the time of mourning. This was the time when sorrow should have filled her heart.

Oddly, it didn't. She felt sad for the wretched life she had lived and the heavy chain of losses she had borne, but she didn't feel the deep heart-wrenching sorrow that mothers felt when their children died. Her eyes were still dry.

The breweress squared her shoulders and stood up. She had no time to analyze. She now had a life that was as close to normal as it would ever get, and she was intent on keeping it this way.

Octavian had ordered a census soon after Cleopatra's magnificent death. He was a shrewd administrator, she would grant him that.

When the census official had arrived at their door, they had given their names as Hera and Helios, of mixed heritage – part Grecian and part Egyptian.

Among the many treasures that Octavian hungered for was the double-crown. He would have found the others, but not the double-crown.

And the last person who could wear it upon his brow was now dead too.

The Ptolemies were dead.

The Pharaohs were dead.

Tears rolled down her cheeks.

She knew that the Egypt of the pharaohs would die soon too.

ᗯᗯᗯ ᑫᑫᑫ ᗯᗯᗯ

Nile rose and fell, again and again.

It rose and fell five times.

Her hair was now beginning to turn gray. The gray hair and the wrinkles were a natural disguise, along with the caustic impression of time upon the memories of people. When she went to the market, she sometimes heard people talk about the

Last Pharaoh and how beautiful she was.

At first, she had found it awkward. Hearing from others the stories of Cleopatra's beauty and her fabulous death, and those sounds of unfelt pity they made by clucking their tongues, made her feel terrible. Then her senses got jaded, and she began to join the conversations about herself – clucking her tongue at the right places.

Now standing in the balcony of her house, she watched the children play. She had borne two with Apollo.

Apollo?

Odd that she should still think of him as Apollo and not Helios. They hadn't called each other with their old names since their arrival here, five years ago. She didn't trust the servants not to overhear, and she couldn't give away this new life that she had built. They were reasonably successful. As successful as they could be without allowing themselves to be seen in the north where the main markets lay.

Mehy was still with them, buried in their backyard. He had rendered her a great service, but after downing a few tumblers of beer, he couldn't be trusted. His life wasn't worth the risk he could become.

"Mother, look she has hit me," her son complained. She looked at them. Her daughter was four and he was about three. Her daughter was like her. Fiercely like her – independent and…Helios called her…*unfeeling*. The girl stood there nonchalantly, unperturbed by the tear-streaked face and the wail of her brother.

Her son looked just like Caesarion did when he was three. He had the same red hair, big eyes, and trusting smile. She knew exactly what he would look like when he grew up, for she still remembered Caesarion.

After Caesarion's birth she hadn't taken Apollo to bed again – not until they had become Helios and Hera. She remembered being worried that Caesar might one day ask her why Caesarion looked more like Apollo than him.

It was a secret that she would take to grave.

A small part of her was glad that she had left that life behind. At least she could have a normal family now.

Hera took a long deep breath and went inside.

The cedar wood trunk was the only thing that she had brought along from her previous life, and since their arrival here it had been sitting in a corner of her bedchamber, untouched and undisturbed.

She won't open it. Not yet. But she would open it once before she died. She could close her eyes and see exactly what she would find inside.

Inside, the *Peschent* or the double crown, lay upon blue silk. It was the crown that her ancestors had worn. It was hers to keep.

Forever.

ᘺᘺᘺ 𝍿𝍿𝍿 ᘺᘺᘺ

Historical Notes:

Cleopatra VII or Cleopatra Philopater was born in 69 BC. Her father Ptolemy XII died after willing that eighteen-year Cleopatra and her ten-year-old brother Ptolemy XIII would jointly rule Egypt.

Cleopatra is credited with the murder of her brothers Ptolemy XIII and Ptolemy XIV.

In 48 BC, twenty-one-year old Cleopatra seduced Julius Caesar by being delivered to him wrapped in a carpet. The deliverer was her confidante Apollodorus.

In 30 BC, Cleopatra committed suicide along with two of her trusted handmaidens Charmion and Iras.

It is debated whether Cleopatra died by consuming poison or because she had herself bitten by a snake.

She also sent a letter to Mark Antony, which made Antony think that she was dead.Upon reading Cleopatra's letter, Mark Antony is said to have fallen upon his sword and committed suicide.

Soon after Cleopatra's death, Octavian killed Caesarion, who Cleopatra had claimed, was the son of Julius Caesar.

An Ancient Egyptian League was about seven miles.

Story Four

THE SPINNER OF DREAMS

~ | New Kingdom – End of Amarna Period | ~

THE SPINNER OF DREAMS

The limestone cliffs that flanked the moonlit *wadi* rose high to kiss the sky, and the landscape was dotted with acacia trees and cacti that threw their deep dark shadows beneath.

On the outskirts of Thebes, at this time of the night, none of the two men expected to be seen.

The man who had driven the chariot held out a bronze cylinder, the kind used for carrying scrolls of importance. The horse-rider took the cylinder and slung it around his neck. The two men stood talking for a few minutes. Then the man, who had arrived in the chariot, jumped into it and rode back toward Thebes. The horse-rider turned his horse away from the city.

In Thebes, the old Pharaoh lay dying.
No tears were shed anywhere by anyone.

〰〰 𓏤𓏤𓏤 〰〰

Nakhtmin returned from his secret appointment and

climbed the steps to Pharaoh Ay's bedchamber. He was not in a hurry. Nothing of import was waiting. Not any more.

"Did he ask for me?" he asked Ankhesenamun, his father Ay's chief royal wife, who was sitting in the antechamber. Her eyes were dry. She hadn't been mourning, but she looked tired, and a lot older than her twenty-five years.

Ankhesenamun smiled without raising her head.

"Could he have?" she answered him with a question.

He knew what she meant, but he also knew that she was an ally. He didn't say anything. Instead he went closer and sat next to her, placing his hand upon hers.

She still didn't look at him.

"He had died before you left, hadn't he?" she asked.

"Do you believe that he had?" Nakhtmin pressed her hand gently.

"Do you think it matters to me?" she chuckled bitterly and pulled her hand away.

He looked at her. There were circles under her eyes, and her cheeks were already sinking. The life she lived was hard and he knew that things would not improve in the short run. Yet Nakhtmin was optimistic that they would eventually change.

"We should not lose hope," he said in an apparent attempt to console her but realized that he was trying to comfort his own distraught heart.

Finally she turned to look at him. Her eyes, tired and puffy, still full of affection for him, fastened to his and she smiled. It was a tired, wry smile.

"It is time we called the Head Priest and others, but before we did, I would like to have a moment with him alone," Nakhtmin said, placing a comforting hand upon her shoulder and went inside.

The Pharaoh's bedchamber looked the stark opposite of his opulent antechamber. It was a large room that had windows opening to a view of the Nile. The walls and the floor were bare. Upon a huge canopied bed, lay the wasted form of Pharaoh Ay. He had been Pharaoh only for three years, and to rule for these three short years, he had waited in the wings for seventy long ones.

The lamps that burned in the wall-sconces threw an eerie glow upon his emaciated face, but the effect was greatly moderated by the single lamp that burned just next to his bed.

He knelt beside the Pharaoh's bed.

"Father," he said, his voice tremulous, "May Anubis's scales be true when your heart is weighed. I can surmise your reasons but I cannot condone your acts, and so I won't answer for you. My *oshabti* that shall accompany you in your afterlife will forever remain silent. Just as I did, all my life."

The Pharaoh listened to him in silence. Nakhtmin wondered if Ay would indeed be concerned with the behavior of Nakhtmin's little wooden figure in the afterlife. Ay had been above such concerns even in this life.

His father lay in calm repose. This had never happened before – that Nakhtmin would speak, and his father would listen.

"I pity your life," Nakhtmin continued, his eyes stinging from the tears he couldn't let through. "You were neither loved nor respected. You were only feared and hated. But it didn't matter to you. I know you died with a smile on your face, because your hardened heart never missed a beat when you paved the road of your success upon the dead dreams of others."

Ay still didn't say a word. He lay there listening to his only son, as the breeze of Nile blew inside his chamber, caressing his dead forehead.

Nakhtmin sat there looking at dark toothless gums inside his father's half-open mouth, he wondered when he had lost those teeth, and thought how painful it must have been to have lost them all, struggling with one pus-filled cavity after another.

"I am sure, you must have felt the pain from your rotting teeth, Father, because it was yours. Your heartlessness never allowed you to feel the pain of your wife or your son, but you weren't immune to your own pain, were you? You must have suffered terribly. You must have even cried out in pain, and I hope that I am right. You didn't deserve to die peacefully in your sleep."

Tears began to fill his eyes again. As he sat there with the dead Pharaoh, memories flooded in. This was the longest he had ever sat with his father.

The sound of the door creaking open brought him back into the present.

"We should inform others," said Ankhesenamun.

Nakhtmin stood up and looked at his father's peaceful countenance one last time. Ankhensenamun's eyes followed his.

"How can he look so peaceful?" she observed.

He knew how.

He had known it for the last fifty years.

᷈᷈᷈ 𓏺𓏺 ᷈᷈᷈

Horemheb rode back from his nocturnal rendezvous. The army had set camp about an hour's ride north from Thebes. The metal cylinder that contained the scroll felt warm and comforting, like the hug of a friend from the afterlife. Horemheb was now nearing fifty, but he was sprightly enough to beat a young soldier in swordplay or engage in pleasure-play with maidens half his age without feeling short of breath.

The scroll had come to him after a long and bloody struggle that he claimed no part in. And yet, he was glad that it was now slung from his neck with its metal-container slapping against his chest, cheering him on.

He had the true pharaoh's blessing - not the pretender's, who now lay dead in the palace, but the one who the pretender had buried three years ago.

Horemheb was in no hurry to reach the camp. The night was dark enough to give him cover, and bright enough to show him the way. He slowed his horse down from a trot to a walk, and allowed his thoughts to meander into the past.

His thoughts however, broke rein and galloped through the landscape of his memories, settling down upon the day he had joined the military, and when as a callow youth, ambitious and energetic, he had the opportunity to save the Pharaoh's life after just about six months in service.

That was more than thirty years ago.

He remembered the time when Pharaoh Amenhotep the Magnificent had, for an inexplicable reason, decided that he wanted to go for a hunt. For any other pharaoh, going on a hunt would have been a normal thing that wouldn't raise any brows, but when the orders came that they must prepare themselves for Pharaoh's hunt, the whole military establishment was awed and shocked.

Pharaoh was not a man one could easily imagine riding a horse or even a chariot and pursuing game. He was an obese man who if weighed, could easily tip the scales against two grown men. To make matters worse, he suffered from weak-knees that wobbled when he walked. True, he was the same man who was credited with the hunt of more than a hundred lions and whose bull-hunt record would never be beaten again by any other pharaoh. And yet, those hunts had happened when Pharaoh was a strapping young man of near about twenty years, not a mammoth heap of squeaky bones and squelching flesh. His second *Heb-sed* celebrating thirty-three years of his reign was being organized in a month's time. While he was not an old man yet, having seen only about forty-five inundations of the Nile, his luxurious, almost sybaritic lifestyle had wreaked havoc upon his body.

Horemheb knew that there were reasons, other than physical, that could make a man go down the path of illness and corpulence. He recalled how a neighbor of his father's had begun draining vats after vats of beer when he had found his wife in bed with his own brother. It had taken that twenty-five-year-old handsome man only a few years to transform into a barrel of fat that couldn't control his farts and would tire from the exertion of taking a bath. The man's wife, with her nose cut as a punishment for her transgression, had changed into a termagant who never left the house. Her loud, shrill voice castigating her husband, however, was heard by the whole neighborhood day and night.

He hadn't known the reasons of Pharaoh's ill health then, for he had seen him only at the festivals, more a figurehead and a deity, than a real person. The announcement of the hunt had made him think about how it would be to meet Pharaoh in person.

The foremost concern of the military was the safety of Pharaoh, and so the Commander had chosen Pharaoh's guard personally. It was by a fortunate chance that Horemheb had found himself among the temporary military elite, who would accompany the Pharaoh on his hunt. His being in the Chariot-division had led them to decide upon him as the Pharaoh's charioteer, and while he was being cheered and envied by others, inside, his guts were in a jumble. He couldn't imagine how it would be to ride on the same footboard as the Pharaoh.

"If only you were thinner, you could have been able to squeeze in," one of his fellow soldiers had made an oblique remark at his supposed good fortune. The footboard of the Egyptian chariot was economically designed to keep the weight of the carriage as low as possible. In this case, he was wondering if some ballast should be added to the carriage to keep it from toppling.

He had gone to the Commander with his suggestion. Unfortunately, Horemheb had caught him at an inopportune moment. The Commander's bath had just been announced, and he was licking his lips and appreciating the nubile body of his new slave boy. While the peasant class's sensibilities were shocked by such perversions, the rich and the royals were above reproach, and so despite his own revulsion, he had stood in front of the Commander, and shared his apprehension.

"Do you have a solution?" the Commander had asked, his eyes still riveted to the back of the boy who sat on the ground polishing the Commander's sword.

Horemheb had suggested adding ballast to the chariot.

"But it would slow him down. Won't it? And he won't like his chariot being slower than those of others."

"Perhaps not, my Lord. But it would keep the chariot from toppling. Right now, it is too light to carry him," he had plodded on.

The Commander's impatience had then bubbled over in form of a veiled threat.

"Are you saying that our dear Pharaoh is too fat and heavy to be riding a chariot?"

Horemheb had escaped from the Commander's tent before their conversation could deteriorate further. While returning to his own tent, he had a strange premonition, an evil one. Something terrible was going to happen the next day. He had no idea what it could be or how he could stop it.

Propitiate the Goddess of Hunting and War, said his inner voice.

And so he had prayed to Neith.

〰 ◊◊◊ 〰

As Nakhtmin sat with the body of his father, memories

that he had tried to bury deep inside his heart found their way into his consciousness.

His life, he thought, *was a string of events that were like wounds.* Some had healed on the inside, but left him scarred; others still festered within. The scars remained etched in his conscience, like milestones upon the path his life had followed. The first event that had scarred him for life had occurred when he was five.

That was forty-five long and wasted years ago.

He remembered peeping into the living chambers of their house, holding both the panels of the curtain tucked under his chin the way children did and felt invisible. The stranger who sat inside looked like an important man. He wore several medallions upon his chest, and sat there upon the *diwan* of their house like he owned the place. Nakhtmin's mother looked like a fragile doll in front of that man.

"Come here," the stranger had noticed his face framed by the curtains and flicked a finger in his direction.

He had stood there frozen. *Why?* He couldn't say. He had felt afraid of the man. He hadn't wanted to leave the protection of the curtain.

But then his mother had smiled at him. He knew his mother's face too well, and he realized that under that smile was a plea.

"Come here, son," she had called.

Her soft voice had taken away some of his terror, and so he had let go of the curtain. Like all the other days, that day too Nakhtmin was wearing a white *shenti* and a simple faience pectoral upon his shoulders. The stranger's eyes swept across his small frame.

"Why is he wearing that rag? And where's his gold-pectoral?" the stranger's voice had boomed deafeningly.

He had lost his courage, and taken a step back.

"Oh, I see. He's a coward as well," the stranger hadn't

missed his attempt to escape.

Nakhtmin had stolen a glance at his mother. It broke his heart to see that she wasn't even looking at him. She was looking down, chewing her lower lip and trying to control her tears.

His mother was young then, he had realized later. She was barely fourteen when she had given birth to him. But he hadn't understood it then and he had expected to find courage through her.

"Come here, boy," the stranger's voice had ordered and he had followed the instruction.

Slowly, he padded upon the carpet and reached his mother. She ignored him and sat there like a stone statue.

The stranger had risen from his seat and plucked him up from his mother's side. Nakhtmin had tried to hold on to her, but she had pried his fingers loose. He had stood trembling in front of the terrifying stranger, when his mother first introduced him to his father.

"Nakht, he is your father," she told him, her voice shaking.

He had heard a lot about his father. He knew that his name was Ay, and he could rattle off his father's titles. He also knew that his father was one of the most important men in Egypt, but this was the first time in his life that he was looking at the man who had sired him.

Standing in front of Ay, he had felt his fear be replaced by awe. He still remembered every detail of that first meeting with his father.

He recalled looking into his father's eyes. Set deep under his bushy brows, they were the gray of granite. His nose was sharp but bent at its tip. His face was gaunt and thin, and so was the rest of his body, and yet, he looked fiercely energetic.

The skin of his face was stretched so tight upon his bones that, Nakhtmin remembered thinking, *if he laughed, he might stretch and tear it.* He hadn't known then that his father never laughed.

"Nakht, kneel before your father and seek his blessings," his mother reminded him.

He had felt afraid, because his father had looked like a vulture, and he didn't want to expose his neck to him. But he had overcome his fear and followed his mother's instruction. He had fallen on his knees and touched his forehead upon the leather sandals that his father wore. Even his feet were thin and ridged.

Ay had blessed him with a critical "hmmm."

When he stood up again and looked up into his eyes, his fear had slipped out of his mouth.

"*Nekhbet*," Nakhtmin had whispered. He had spoken the name of the vulture-god because that was exactly how Ay appeared to him. Anyone else would have ignored it as the senseless babble of a five-year-old, but not Ay.

To Ay, everything mattered.

"What did you say, my son?" he had asked, sweetening his voice and goading him to say it again. Had he looked upon his mother's face then, he would have seen her warning him, asking him to say nothing. But he hadn't looked at his mother, and gone on to repeat the word.

"*Nekhbet*," he had repeated it again, innocent and hopeful that his father might thump his back for his observation and creativity.

But his father's cold gray eyes had turned grayer as his pupil shrunk to a point.

"You think that I look like a vulture?" Ay had asked.

In his innocence, he had nodded.

That had sent Ay into a sort of seizure. He laughed until tears came out of his eyes.

"Quite a compliment, son. Perhaps I have the divine element of *Nekhbet* in me, and one day, I'll rule Egypt," he had told him.

Then he had asked him about his training, and told him to focus on swordplay and archery. He had said a few more things, which Nakhtmin couldn't recall now. Then he was dismissed.

He remembered feeling elated when his father had asked him to go. He had felt like he was suddenly set free. He remembered running out of the living room, never sparing a thought for his mother.

The man, who had come home a stranger and then changed into his father, had stayed that night in his mother's bedroom. They used to live in Thebes then, in their grandfather's house. He remembered his grandfather and grandmother too. When he thought about them, warmth spread through his heart, making him feel comfortable and protected. Just the opposite of what his father had made him feel.

So the man had stayed, and given him his next memory.

He had heard the scuffle in the night. Theirs was a rich family, which meant that the children didn't sleep in the same room as their parents, but because his father was never home, he had continued sleeping in his mother's bed. That night, despite all the tantrums he had thrown, his mother had made him sleep in a different room.

"I'll be next door," she had consoled him. "But he is my husband and when he is home, I must sleep with him."

"But I don't want to leave you alone with that vulture-man," he had told her in his brave five-year-old voice.

His mother had hugged him and placed a kiss on his forehead. He felt a slight wetness upon his cheek, which he later realized, was due to her tears.

"Nakht," she had twiddled his nose and smiled, "I'll be safe. And this isn't permanent. You'll sleep in my room again, but you will have to wait for him to go away."

"I hope that he goes away now, and never comes back," he had grumbled.

"Don't say that, Nakht. He is your father," his mother had shushed him. Then she had tucked him in and left, closing the door softly behind her.

He had tried hard to sleep but his vulture-faced father had kept bouncing in and out of his dreams. First he saw him as a man with the beak of a vulture and the teeth of a crocodile. Then Ay turned into a snake with big yellow eyes. Next he was squatting upon his mother trying to throttle her.

The last one had him sitting up in his bed and whimpering. It was then that he had heard the sounds.

They were spilling into his room from his mother's. He could hear her sniffling and crying. She sounded as if she were in pain. Then there were those other sounds that he couldn't place. He hadn't heard them ever before.

He had crawled down his bed and crept out of his room. There was still light in his mother's room. He peeked through the space between the two panes of the door and saw what his mother had never wanted him to see. But what he had seen, he could never erase, and so the memory had stuck.

Nakhtmin had seen his mother crouched naked upon the floor, while his father, the man who he had never seen until this afternoon, was whipping her.

"That boy is a coward," Ay screamed at his mother, "he cannot be mine!"

His mother mumbled something that was unintelligible to him, but it happened to calm his father down.

"We'll see then. Let him grow up into a strong man and prove to me that he is my son!"

Then the man, his father, had kneeled by her side and said something to her, after which she had stopped crying, gone to her bed, and lain down. Nakhtmin saw the man remove his belt and drop his *shenti*, and realized that it might not be something that his mother would want him to watch.

So he had returned to his own room and bed.

He hadn't slept that night, for he knew that the next morning would dawn differently. What he had hoped for, however, was that the man who was his father would be gone by the time he woke up.

Horus, make him go away. He is a creature of Seth and you are Seth's vanquisher, so I know that you can make him go away. Please don't let him kill my mother, O' Horus, he had kept praying until he fell asleep.

∿∿ 𓏤𓏤𓏤 ∿∿

Horemheb remembered that the day of the hunt had dawned busy with excitement, for the Pharaoh's hunt was not an everyday affair. It would result in hundreds of beasts being hunted and brought back for the feast. The antelopes, the ostriches, the gazelles, the hyenas, the leopards and the lions were all game, and while the lions and leopards weren't now as abundant as the used to be, the Master of the Hunt would have secured some from the South, to ensure that Pharaoh had an opportunity to improve his personal score of a hundred and two lions.

First, there was the sacrificial ceremony. The ox had already been chosen and sealed by the priests, and now they were chanting the verses that would awaken the gods, specifically Neith, the goddess of hunting and war, to partake the sacrifice and bless the hunt.

It was during the ceremony that Horemheb had first laid eyes upon Pharaoh. He was nothing like he had imagined him to be. Dressed in the hunter's kilt that was covered with a leather-guard designed to protect the King's most valued jewels, he wore a crocodile skin breastplate like the rest of them. His leather sandals were secured with leather-bands crisscrossing to cover his thick legs below the knees. The only part that remained uncovered and unprotected and which offered a humungous target to anyone meaning to bring him harm, was his fleshy brown belly.

For the ceremony, Pharaoh had chosen to wear the blue crown of war. Under the crown, his forehead was full of worry-lines. His eyes, now beady and receding into their sockets, had bags under them, and his many jowls had pushed his chin and neck into obscurity. All in all, he looked like an oversized incarnation of *Bes,* the dwarf god.

He had quickly averted his eyes upon realizing that he was staring at Pharaoh, and tried focusing upon the others.

On the left side of Pharaoh, stood Horemheb's *nuk*-loving Commander, but Horemheb's attention had been arrested by the gaunt and tall middle-aged man, who stood at the right of Pharaoh. The man was the stark opposite of Pharaoh in the way he looked and moved. He was as thin as a desiccated reed and as sprightly as a horse.

"That's Ay, the Grand Vizier," the soldier standing next to Horemheb had whispered.

He had heard about Ay, and that his history with the royalty went back a few generations. His most important link to Pharaoh was his sister Tiye, the chief royal wife of Pharaoh. This link meant that Ay was the brother-in-law of Pharaoh, and from what he had heard, Ay spent more time in the royal palace than his own.

Reminded of Pharaoh, he looked at him once again.

How will he hunt? He thought, his mind groaning under a deluge of possibilities. There were so many ways that things could go wrong, and if anything happened to Pharaoh, he would be held responsible.

After the ceremony had ended, the priest came out with a bowl and smeared the ox's blood upon the shoulders of all those present at the ceremony.

The hunt was to take place in the royal preserve, where the peasants weren't allowed to enter, and the nobles needed permission to hunt. It was a forest that kept the animals in, where lured by a false sense of freedom, they gathered around the waterholes fed by the Nile.

The hunt had begun soon after the ceremony had ended. The hunters were a patient lot. They knew about the habits of the animals, and had already positioned themselves at the vantage points they considered the best.

As Pharaoh's charioteer Horemheb had maneuvered the chariot behind a pile of rocks from where they had a clear view of the waterhole.

Pharaoh had addressed him soon after they had reached there.

"What is your name?" he had asked him. Standing in such close proximity to Egypt Incarnate was already making Horemheb conscious. When he heard Pharaoh's voice, he nearly jumped out of his skin.

"Horemheb, Your Majesty," he had mustered all his courage and replied with dignity.

"Hmm," Pharaoh had considered his name for a moment and then asked him again.

"Which family do you come from?"

Horemheb found it odd that a man must be weighed by the name of his family, and he would have ignored the question, had the man asking him, not been Pharaoh.

"None that you would know of, Your Majesty," he had replied. His eyes concentrating upon the waterhole and his ears pinned behind to listen to the sounds. *Nothing out of place there yet,* he thought*, just the birds and the insects.*

"None? Then your skills must have earned you a place in the hunt. I am glad they didn't pin a miserable pedigreed excuse of a soldier upon me. Everyone I ever meet these days is a brother or a son of someone I know," Pharaoh gave a hearty laugh.

Horemheb had never expected Pharaoh to possess a sense of humor. He found himself warming toward the man.

"They will begin to gather here in a moment," Pharaoh said, pointing to a lone deer that was cautiously approaching the water.

Horemheb looked at Pharaoh. He had the eager look of a young man out to enjoy a hunt, confident in his ability to steer even the direst of situations in his favor. His eyes shone in anticipation of the hunt.

The deer were gathering on one side of the watering hole. On the other side, a lone leopard moved through the grass. He would move surreptitiously in the hope of catching its prey unaware, little realizing that an arrow waited nocked and ready, on the opposite side, in the dense foliage behind the pile of rocks.

Pharaoh had his eyes fastened upon the svelte frame of the leopard. He was waiting for the creature to turn sideways and expose its belly. That would give him a bigger target and a surer shot. Horemheb was surprised at how steady Pharaoh's aim was. It would have been better had they been off the chariot, but his instructions were to keep Pharaoh safe, and he would be safest riding upon a pair of wheels drawn by the two fastest horses in the kingdom.

So Horemheb waited and prayed that the horses will remain quiet until Pharaoh's arrow had found its mark.

He heard the twang of the bow, the neighing of the horses, and the roar of the lion behind them, in the same instant. The horses had felt the presence of the master predator a moment before it had roared. Horemheb was pleasantly surprised to see that his rider was nonplussed. He was nocking another arrow, in the direction of the lion.

Horemheb's premonition returned with a staggering force, making him lose control of his thoughts for a moment, but he quickly regained his composure. The horses had reared and he had to rein them in.

"Your Majesty," he shouted, forgetting that he was addressing Pharaoh, "hold on to the edge."

The horses followed his cue and their front legs came down upon the ground. He urged the horses and they shot away from the lion. Horemheb who was keeping an eye on his fare, watched with horror as he saw Pharaoh lose his foothold, become airborne, and topple out of the carriage.

The horses galloped away, taking Horemheb away from Pharaoh, who was sprawled upon the ground and shrinking in size every moment. Terrorized, he realized the magnitude of his folly. The round shiny ball rolling in the dirt was Egypt himself. He was Amenhotep the Magnificent, and if he lost Pharaoh, he would lose not only his job but also his life.

He looked around frantically. On his left was a clearing where he could turn the chariot without stopping. He pulled the left reins in, and the horses turned, still galloping. In a moment, they had deposited him by Pharaoh's side, and gone on ahead. He and Pharaoh now together faced the lion.

The hunters had in moments become the hunted. Those were the ways of fate.

He now stood by the side of the greatest lion-hunter in the history of Egypt, who was sweating and panting, and yet trying to keep his demeanor. Pharaoh still had his bow, but his arrows were now scattered all around. Horemheb had nothing except his sword. His only chance was to wait for the lion to attack.

But they stood together. Pharaoh and Horemheb. And if the lion reasoned it out the way humans did, he would go for the bigger target.

"Horus, spread your wings and protect us," he prayed under his breath then slowly and deliberately, setting protocol aside, he spoke to Pharaoh.

"Majesty, please step back very slowly. Whiplash me later for my impertinence, but right now, do as I ask."

Pharaoh Amenhotep the Magnificent, perhaps for the first time in his life, followed an instruction. He began stepping back, slowly and soundlessly.

The lion watched the play, its eyes flickering with interest. And then, in a moment, it was airborne. It had decided to go after the bigger target after all. Horemheb saw the moment, and responded to it instantly. Crouching, he pointed his sword upward and shoved it up into the belly of the beast. The lion roared deafeningly as it lost its momentum and turned in the air, falling down right where Horemheb had stood moments earlier. As the lion turned to its side, it revealed Horemheb's sword, half its blade buried in its chest. It had entered at an angle below the sternum and plunged into its heart.

Behind him, Pharaoh nocked an arrow that he had picked off the ground, and let it fly.

"Better make sure, it's dead. I know. I've killed many of these beasts in my time," said Pharaoh. It was, as in the last hour, he had suddenly grown old.

Horemheb watched Pharaoh – a giant among men, stood a broken man today, and realized that he didn't want to be the savior of Amenhotep the Magnificent.

The sounds of chariots and horses and men were quickly filling up the air that surrounded them. They must have heard the roar of the lion.

Horemheb bent down and closing both his hands upon the hilt of his sword, he pulled it out and cleaned it with the dirt. Only Pharaoh's arrow with its tail proudly displaying the single feather of an eagle remained embedded in the lion's chest.

When he had cleaned his sword and returned it to the scabbard, he felt Pharaoh's hand upon his shoulder.

ᴧᴧᴧ ۩۩۩ ᴧᴧᴧ

Incense burners had been placed around the dead Pharaoh's bed. The priests too had arrived and they had begun to plan the rites that had to be completed before Pharaoh Ay's body was transported to his funerary temple for mummification.

Nakhtmin knew that he had to be part of every ritual there was. He was Ay's only son, and despite his own feelings on the matter, he had to do many things that he didn't want to.

He had a secret that he had never shared with anyone. *He had hated his father all his life.*

Ay had terrorized his mother and he had attempted to instill the same fear in Nakhtmin's own heart. Ay believed that a man must be strong and ruthless, shrewd and cunning, and that a man should never be hurt by anything.

Nakhtmin was none of this. He had taken after his mother, and that had been unacceptable to his father. Fortunately, when Nakhtmin was a child, Ay didn't live with them. He thought it politically opportune to live in the royal palace with his sister Tiye and his brother-in-law, Pharaoh Amenhotep. Living in the royal household enabled him to influence Pharaoh's decisions, and Ay was a crafty and ambitious man, with little love for his son and his son's mother.

At nine, Nakhtmin had discovered his calling. He had learned that he wanted to be a painter and a scribe, for he loved the logical beauty of the hieroglyphs. Being the son of Ay, he was never in want of anything material, including his access to education. He had four different tutors, and he was told that the two most important skills that he needed to learn were military strategy and weapon wielding. The other two tutors taught him writing and languages. He knew that his father wanted him to be good at archery and swordplay. His mother, who feared his father, would remind him of it, whenever she got a chance.

Nakhtmin loved his mother. She was a sweet and kind woman. If he reflected upon her virtues and weaknesses objectively, he could have added the adjectives mousy and scared too, but as her son he found it difficult to think about his mother objectively. For him, she was the best mother in the world. More than anything else, he wanted to please her. But despite his efforts, his performance in the desired areas remained poor.

When his masters told his mother that he was good at languages and writing, but terrible in wielding weapons and proposing strategies, her eyes had grown big with fear.

"You must not be teaching him properly," she had accused his swordplay and archery tutor. "He is Ay's son," she had added, like she thought that calling him Ay's son could magically instill in him the skills he lacked.

"Not everyone is born to wield weapons of war, some are meant to change the world with their knowledge," his teacher had tendered.

His mother had looked a little confused, but when his teacher had explained that Nakhtmin was a precocious child who could become a scholar in his own right, she had warmed up to the thought. She was still worried about Ay's reaction, but she saw a ray of hope, and so she spoke to Nakhtmin about it.

"Son," she took him into her arms and seated him on her lap, "you don't like swordplay and archery, do you?"

He shook his head vehemently. He hated the mindlessness of it. "I don't like hunting either," he told her.

"So what is it that you like?" she asked.

"I love to read, write, and paint," he had replied. There was no ambiguity in his reply. Both he and his mother knew that his father wanted the opposite. The scene between his mother and father that he had witnessed years ago was seared deep into his memory. He couldn't lie to his mother. If she wanted him to try and become good at being a soldier, he would try…*for her.*

"I'll do what you want me to," he had told her, simply and truthfully. His mother had hugged him tight. So tight that he had trouble breathing, but before he started struggling she loosened her grip and turned his face to her.

"Nakht," she said, biting back her tears, "I want you to do what you love doing. You won't understand it now, but sacrificing your happiness for anyone, even for your parents, is not the right thing to do. Your life is yours to live. You have a finite number of days to live, and you do not know how many. You must spend them wisely upon doing what you like best. You don't owe it to anyone."

"When I was little," she continued, "a learned man had once visited our house. He had said something that I have always remembered, even though I often didn't have the courage to stand by it. He said that we don't choose our gods, our gods choose us. You are *Thoth*'s chosen one, and if you defy him to follow *Menthu*, *Thoth* won't let you go and *Menthu* won't accept you as his own. You'll forever be torn between the two."

"So, follow your heart, Nakht," she had kissed his head, "I will stand up to your father."

And she had. In all the years that followed she had stood by her son. Her opposition to his diktats had led Ay to reject her. He had even threatened to go to the council and accuse her of adultery, but she hadn't wavered. In her own mousy way, she had clung to her son's dreams. He may have whipped her again, for disobedience, disloyalty, or for any other imaginary transgression, but Nakhtmin had never learned about it.

He had given himself to a study of everything. He studied the treatises that were compiled by different scribes of Egypt and Syria in the last thousand years. He learned about political and military strategy, geography, mining methods, even mathematics. And he learned the hieroglyphs – all of them, with all their interpretations.

Those were the years that he loved.
Those were the times when he was at peace.

His peace was shattered when they moved to the city of *Aten*, Akhet-aten, which was built by Akhenaten the Heretic, who was the son of Amenhotep the Magnificent. Amenhotep was succeeded by his son, the fourth of his name, who had disowned the old gods and replaced them with one god *Aten* the sun disk. He had changed his own name to Akhenaten, which meant the successor of *Aten*.

In the newly built city of Akhet-aten, the stranger started living with Nakhtmin and his mother.

ᴡᴡᴡ 𓂀𓂀𓂀 ᴡᴡᴡ

Among Horemheb's clearest memories was that of the hunt. For the first time in his life, something special had happened to him.

When they had returned from the hunt, praises of Pharaoh Amenhotep the Magnificent filled the air. His prowess, the lack of which was often discussed behind his back, was now firmly established. The man, who could kill a lion at his age, could not be merely a man, he had to be divine.

Pharaoh, who had almost forgotten what such adulation felt like, was delighted by the attention. The sumptuous feast that followed, served the meat brought in by the hunters. Pharaoh, who had left his palace after a very long time, sat outside his tent with his officials, while exotic dancers danced to the music that the royal musicians played.

Everyone looked happy, except the Grand Vizier Ay, whose crestfallen expression belied the agony of his heart. It was clear that Ay was unhappy about something. When Horemheb's eyes fell upon him, he was looking in the direction of Pharaoh, and his face was set in a frown. As Ay was looking elsewhere, Horemheb, who was sitting with the other soldiers, took another opportunity to study his features.

Ay's thinness was extraordinary. Everything about him was thin and long. His nose, slightly crooked was thin from its bridge to its tip; his face was oval; his ears were long too, which was a sign of longevity. And that was just his face. He was tall and slim. His body appeared to be made entirely of thin long lines and vertically elongated planes.

Horemheb was lost in looking at Ay's profile, when the subject of his scrutiny turned, very suddenly, and looked straight into his eyes. Horemheb was taken aback, but he held his gaze, until Ay looked away, slowly and deliberately. Not a word had passed between them, but he had instinctively known that Ay had marked him for a purpose of his own.

The next morning Pharaoh Amenhotep had promoted Horemheb and placed around his neck the medallion of the Golden Lion and commended him for his bravery.

But what had taken him completely by surprise was a visit by Ay. He was at his modest house in Thebes, when Ay had alighted from his litter and strode into his antechamber.

"Pharaoh wants you to marry my daughter Mudjemnet," he had stated in his staid and direct manner.

Horemheb remembered being flabbergasted. He was married then to Amenia, and quite in love with her, and he hadn't spared a thought to marrying again, ever in his life.

"Think about it for a day," Ay had told him. "If the proposal doesn't meet your approval, let me know, and I will inform Pharaoh."

Ay hadn't stayed for refreshments.

"I can't make Pharaoh wait for me, can I?" he had told young Horemheb when he had insisted.

Horemheb had found the whole incident quite disturbing. He was in love with his wife, and being a common Egyptian, he had found the idea of marrying a second time, rather unacceptable. So had talked to his wife Amenia about it.

She had asked him to accept the proposal.

"But why?" he had asked her.

"Because the marriage will connect you to the royalty," she told him. "Even a tenuous connection to the royalty could help your fortunes. Mudjemnet is not only Ay's daughter but also the sister of Nefertiti, and Nefertiti is the favorite wife of our crown prince. After Pharaoh Amenhotep leaves this world for the next, his son shall be Pharaoh, and you will be the husband of Queen Nefertiti sister."

Amenia's understanding of complex relationships that existed within the Egyptian royalty far exceeded Horemheb's own, and she was brilliant at understanding human nature.

"You have to hear the unsaid and see what Ay keeps hidden. Pharaoh likes you. Perhaps he even wanted you to marry one of his daughters. He would have slept easier in the nights knowing that you would be there to counter the influence of Ay upon the crown prince."

Horemheb found the thought interesting.

"You think that Pharaoh Amenhotep might have considered a marriage between me and one of his daughters?" he asked.

Amenia had laughed. "Maybe, maybe not. Don't let it go to your head. But Ay would never want you to come directly in the line of ascension, and so he must have proposed his own daughter Mutnedjmet's name instead. By refusing, you'll be playing in Ay's hands, for he would distort it all for the Pharaoh's ear."

That sounded plausible and very characteristic of Ay. And so, much to Ay's chagrin, he had accepted the proposal.

He had wedded Mutnedjmet in a simple ceremony that was held in the royal grounds. That was the night that he had first seen Nakhtmin.

When Nakhtmin had approached the couple and sprinkled upon them the water of Nile, the priest had announced his name and relationship to his new wife Mutnedjmet.

Nakhtmin was Mutnedjmet's half-brother.

Horemheb still remembered how beautiful and vulnerable Nakhtmin had looked that evening.

At that time, Nakhtmin must have been no more than sixteen. He was as tall as his father, but that was where the similarities ended. Unlike Ay, Nakhtmin's face was soft, his nose though aquiline didn't bend at its tip, and his beautiful eyes, bigger than his father's, were not hidden under the shadow cast by his eyebrows. His irises were a strangely exotic mix of green and blue, and they looked at everything with wonder. Nakhtmin didn't wear his hair braided on one side, as was the custom among the pureblood Egyptians, instead his golden brown curls danced in the breeze that blew through the gardens, ostensibly to bless the new couple.

When the boy had walked toward them, carrying the small ceremonial pitcher of Nile water, Horemheb had been able to think of only one word that could describe Nakhtmin.

Ethereal.

That image had remained in his mind all these years. Even now, when Nakhtmin was nearing fifty, he still had that willowy grace, and while his hair had turned gray, they still danced in the breeze.

〰 𓏥 〰

Queen Ankhesenamun, the Chief Royal Wife of the dead Pharaoh, had taken it upon herself to inform the harem that Pharaoh Ay was dead.

Nakhtmin could imagine how the women must have

responded to the news. Most must have turned their side and gone back to sleep. Some might have taken this as an opportunity to garner material for gossip – and there may have been a few who would have smiled and said a small prayer to their patron god or goddess, hoping that they would now get a Pharaoh who shall pull Egypt out of the hole it was in now.

He knew that his father had died unloved, and he also knew that Ay didn't care to be loved.

As Nakhtmin went through Pharaoh Ay's personal effects, looking for anything that could deliver a shattering blow to his plans later, anything that his devious father might have left to be found after his death – another will, even a piece of parchment that could ignite suspicion in the minds of people.

Nakhtmin would not let his father's last wish come true!

He slid the last drawer in his father's armoire open.

Inside he found a roll of papyri that looked faintly familiar. With his heart beating against his chest, he picked it up and carried it to his father's table. Placing it in the circle of light that the lamp threw upon the table, he unrolled it, his fingers trembling.

They were letters written in Nakhtmin's own hand. Each glyph carefully drawn, these were the letters that he had searched for, for thirty long years.

They were the letters in which Nakhtmin had poured his heart out to Merkhet.

Nuk…nuk…nuk!

Ay's voice still boomed in his head.

Nuk…nuk…nuk!

His thoughts were shoving him into places and times that he had been trying to forget for years.

Thirty-five long years – since he first learned the truth that would change his life forever.

He had always known that he was different, but hadn't known how. He had no idea what other boys his age did, but all his interactions with them strengthened his belief that he was different.

His friends talked about women, and spoke about them in ways that he found repelling. He could never imagine being with a woman the way they described.

Women reminded him of his mother.

"How can you even think of it?" he had once asked his friend.

"You never think of it?" his friend had shot back with a question that had made him wonder.

Why did his friends stare at women with such longing?
What did they feel for women that he didn't?

He had been sixteen when, for the first time in his life, he had seriously considered the question.

Oddly, the two most important events in his life happened almost at the same time, and it all began on the day of Horemheb and Mutnedjmet's wedding.

He had been sixteen when his half-sister Mutnedjmet had got married to Horemheb. That was the first time he had seen Horemheb, the young man who had been dominating the palace grapevine since the fabled hunt. Nakhtmin and others, especially the young girls in the palace, had conjured images of a handsome young man wearing the Gold Lion upon his chest. None of them had seen him, but the facts that he had just crossed twenty and had been awarded the highest medal of bravery in Egypt, were sufficient to set everyone's imagination on fire.

They were all in for a terrible disillusionment.

When Nakhtmin had first looked at his half-sister's husband, he was shocked.

Horemheb was a short and stout man with bulging muscles that made him look shorter. The ridge of his forehead jutted out, giving him an ape-like appearance. His eyes however, were his redeeming feature, for they were honest and trusting.

Nakhtmin had remembered Horemheb's eyes.

He had remembered the honesty in his eyes with hope, and the trust, with fear.

After the wedding, the couple went into the chamber that had been specially prepared for them to consummate their marriage. As the guests waited outside the chamber, they bantered, their jokes quickly turning ribald, for the ceremony of red flower was an opportunity for the elite to have some proletarian fun.

They had all been standing there for a little more than an hour, drinking wine and laughing, when the door opened and Horemheb walked out with the white bed-sheet. He shook it open and spread it for all to see.

The red flower of the bride was impressed upon the white linen. It was the size of a rose, and looked like one.

Nakhtmin had been watching it with such interest that he nearly jumped out of his skin when he heard his mother's voice.

"You too will soon be married, and your bride's flower would be even more beautiful. She will give you many sons," his mother said, her eyes dreamy.

Her remark had made him anxious, because unlike his friends, he felt nothing for women.

He hadn't been able to sleep that night. The next morning, he had shared his concern with his closest friend Merkhet who had suggested that he should accompany him to a love-temple.

He had heard about the love-temples or the pleasure houses, but never having entered one, he eagerly accompanied Merkhet. He was curious of what he might experience there, and whether he too would come back bubbling with excitement like his friends did.

Perhaps, he too would get one of those dreams that will make him hard and stiff, and make him resemble *Min* the god of male virility who was often depicted holding his erect penis in his left hand.

He knew that the stiffness of their member was highly desirable among men, for without the stiffening, the seed wouldn't come forth. He had gathered that women were instrumental in bringing about this monumental change in the male member, causing the soft and innocuous organ to change in shape and volume and become a symbol of power and fertility.

Nakhtmin remembered the incident that one of his friends had shared with him. His friend had dreamed of not one or two, but three beautiful women who had raised his stele high, and then when one of those love-goddesses had straddled him, making him feel like *Min* himself, his mother had thrown a bucket of water on him and woken him up!

Everyone had found the incident funny, except Nakhtmin.

It wasn't that he hadn't experienced the stiffening, but it wasn't anything like what his friends had described.

When he first set foot in one of the streets that he had always avoided, he was mesmerized by the colors that he saw. These houses, if they could be called that, were different from the ones elsewhere, for each house here had a single chamber with just one door, one window, and a bed. In each open window burned an earthen lamp and in each open door stood a woman who wore nothing but faience beads on her body and a blue amulet upon her forehead.

The women all looked beautiful with their lips red with ochre. Their bodies varied, from plump to thin and from tall to short. Men who walked the streets, stopped and talked to the woman they liked and paid her before going inside and closing the door. The sounds that filled the street were a concoction of the soft giggles of women and the husky hoarse whispers of men. Most chambers had incense burning inside and the women wore perfumes.

"It's beautiful here," Nakhtmin observed to his friend.

"Beautiful?" Merkhet laughed. "You haven't seen beauty yet."

They kept walking until they had covered at least half the length of the street. The houses were now bigger and better maintained.

Merkhet stopped in front of a house that had its walls painted blue.

"They are the best," Merkhet said, bending his head and entering. He told Nakhtmin that he had already paid for both of them to spend the night there.

Nakhtmin followed his friend in and realized that Merkhet was right. He had never seen such a place before.

The antechamber was itself a work of art. Unlike the funerary and temple art, here the walls were filled with realistic imagery of men and women copulating in different positions, but they all had the same expression of ecstasy on their faces. Somewhere within, music was being played.

"This is one of the best pleasure houses in the city. They employ harpists, lute-players, singers, and dancers. Here, the music never stops," explained Merkhet.

Nakhtmin nodded. The allure of the place was already beginning to work its magic on him.

"This is what you will experience tonight, my friend," Merkhet had tapped his shoulder and pointed to a painting that depicted two women and a man.

"Two? I don't know what I would be doing with one," he fumbled with his words, already feeling nervous.

"Everyone learns," said Merkhet, signaling him to follow, as he went into the aisle. The aisle was flanked on both sides with doors that looked nearly alike, except that they had numbers painted upon them.

"This is our room," he said, stopping at one of the doors and knocking.

The door opened immediately. It was clear that the inmates were expecting their visitors.

The woman who opened the door was in her early thirties. Her full bare breasts had large dark aureoles that glistened with perfumed oil. Around her waist, she wore only a belt that had strings of faience beads hanging from it. Her complexion was brown with a tinge of copper, which quite like her full body and well-formed hips, tattled of her mixed heritage.

"*Hilsu* with cinnamon," he remarked, breathing in a lung-full of the air within.

"You are the first man to recognize our perfume," the woman commented. "Most of our guests are like your friend here," she pointed to Merkhet.

He had turned to look at Merkhet and saw that his eyes were riveted to the woman's thighs and beads of sweat were already beginning to appear on his forehead. Something was happening to Merkhet, which meant that something should have been happening to him too.

But he felt nothing.

He looked at the other woman in the room. She was younger and clearly all Egyptian. She was lighter in complexion, yet her coloring was a brown that was deeper than the desert sand. She lay upon a linen sheet that was dyed the color of wine and heightened her sensuality. She wore nothing except armlets and anklets.

Merkhet was by now already in the thralls of the older woman. He was holding her body against his, and squeezing her breasts and belly, as they straggled to the bed. The woman giggled continuously as she kneaded Merkhet's hips in an attempt to return the favor.

Nakhtmin watched her hands spellbound and felt a stir under his belly.

The young woman who was lying on the bed realized that something was amiss. Perhaps she had expected him to behave the same as Merkhet and pounce upon her like she was a piece of meat and he, a hungry lion.

She rose from the bed, and walked toward him.

She had a sensuous walk, or a walk that most men found sensuous. Her hips undulated as she sashayed toward him. Her breasts bounced slightly, almost like they were dancing to the music that was softly wafting in from outside. Her skin was smooth and unblemished. He should have wanted to touch it, but he didn't. He enjoyed the show for its artistry, but he didn't feel anything. He heard no sound of blood rushing in his ears; he felt no tightening of his loins; neither did he experience any uncontrollable desire! He loved the display, the music, the visual treat – but all it had made him want to do was compose a poem.

The woman came nearer and smiled.

"Come with me," she said, holding his hand, pulling him along.

He went with her. He had promised himself that he would swim along with the current, because if he didn't let her do what she wanted, how could he ever hope to experience what his friends had?

So he let her throw him on the bed and touch him everywhere. She ran her fingers across his chest, over his stomach, and then she unhooked his *shenti*. On the other side of the bed, Merkhet had already stripped naked, and between his legs his stele had already grown in girth and length. It looked magnificent, making him wonder how lovely it would be to…

And then Merkhet touched himself.

Nakhtmin felt his first strong surge of excitement.

The young woman, who was intent upon him, had noticed it too.

"We too will get there soon enough," she remarked following Nakhtmin's eyes.

He tore his eyes away from Merkhet's magnificence and tried to concentrate upon the attractive curvaceous woman who was sitting upon his thighs. Her young breasts were glistening with the pearls of her labor and between her own thighs was ensconced his own meager tool. Unwilling to rise to the occasion, it was beginning to flag.

He stole another glance at Merkhet. The woman was on her knees and elbows and her generous hips were offered to appease Merkhet's monster, which reared its head like a cobra ready to strike. Nakhtmin suddenly found himself rising and rushing, wanting and seeking release. He felt his own hips clenching and relaxing in response to Merkhet's strokes.

The young woman felt rewarded for her efforts as she positioned herself upon him, allowing him to enter, coming down upon him, letting her breasts touch his chest, and blocking his view of his friend's passionate lovemaking.

Nakhtmin felt himself go limp inside the woman whose attempts to fake pleasure were suddenly cut short, as he slipped out of her. As he heard the sounds of release from the other bed, he felt a wave of jealousy envelop him.

He was jealous of the woman who lay under Merkhet.
He wished he were in her place.

Later, he had felt saddened by the whole episode, for he hated hurting people, and he was sure that he had insulted that young love-priestess by not responding to her. Though the insult wasn't deliberate, he fretted over it for a whole week.

The episode hadn't ended well for Nakhtmin, and yet it hadn't been entirely fruitless. He had learned something about himself.

Unfortunately, his discovery had left him a broken man. He would have stayed broken had Merkhet not seen and understood.

"You desire me," he had asked him when they were returning from their rendezvous.

"Did those women say something to you?" he asked, worried that the secret that he had just discovered about himself might be leaked.

He would be destroyed if it did.

"The women didn't say anything. Your eyes did all the talking. When you were watching me, I was watching your eyes," Merkhet had replied, his own voice shaking a little.

Suddenly it had become very important for him to know what Merkhet thought about him.

"Do you hate me?" he asked.

"Hate you for desiring me?" Merkhet had stopped and looked in Nakhtmin's eyes. "Go home and look at yourself. You are beautiful. More beautiful than all those women you saw there," he had told him. Then his eyes softening, Merkhet had said the words that he would never forget.

"I love you, Nakht," he had whispered, his voice turning hoarse with emotion.

"Just me, or others too?" he had asked, his voice quivering and cheeks flushing. Nakhtmin was suddenly anxious - worried about sharing his lover's affection, like a woman might be. He wanted to be the only one Merkhet loved.

"I love being with women, but I don't love them. I love you. I've always loved you, but I never had the courage to tell you. You are Grand Vizier Ay's son. What if you weren't the way you are? You may have hated me for even suggesting that I wanted you the way I…wanted women. Tonight, I too wished for you to have been in her place."

Merkhet was right. To be desired by a man and to become a receptacle of his seed was considered to be the most terrible fate that could befall a man. Such a man would be derided as a *nuk;* never to be considered a true man again.

And yet, Merkhet had given wings to his dreams, for there was nothing that he wanted more than to be taken by Merkhet, who was his friend, his confidante, and who would soon become his lover.

They spent that night together in Nakhtmin's own

chambers, and for the first time in his life, he experienced the release that he had always dreamed of.

The next morning, everyone he met appeared to be looking at him differently. He looked at their faces and wondered whether they had somehow learned about his secret. But in time, the feeling had gone away.

Nakhtmin had fallen in love.

He had fallen in love with the man who understood him and loved him for what he was. It was true that Merkhet had a family. In time, Nakhtmin would have one too. But that didn't stop them from finding happiness with each other, for that was how they were made. Nakhtmin knew that his life would be destroyed if anyone learned about them.

Merkhet was merely doing what many already did. They had a wife and they liked men and women both. It was quite common for nobles to keep young boys to satisfy their carnal desires of the other kind.

The problem was that…*Nakhtmin was that young boy.*

It was the ultimate humiliation – the humiliation that *Seth* had wanted to inflict upon his nephew *Horus* when he had tried to rape him.

Seth, who was envious of his brother Osiris, had killed him in a battle, hacked his body into numerous pieces, which he then threw away. Isis who was their sister and Osiris's wife had then gone looking for Osiris's body parts so that she could assemble them and make her husband whole. Unfortunately, she hadn't been able to find his member, and so she had fashioned one from wood and then impregnated herself through it with her dead husband's seed.

Horus was born of that divine union, but his uncle Seth, who still nurtured his hatred for Osiris, now wanted to demean and insult his brother's son Horus, and to achieve this, he had planned upon raping young Horus. Horus, however, caught his uncle's seed in his hand and took it to his mother Isis. Upon learning of her evil brother's designs, Isis immediately cut off Horus's hand, which grew back for he was divine. Horus collected his own seed in the lettuce leaves and tricked Seth into consuming it. Seth who had thus ingested Horus's seed not only became subservient to Horus, but also the laughing stock of the gods.

The lore, in its several different versions, was etched in the mind of all Egypt.

The man, who received another's seed in his body, was worse than a woman.

Nakhtmin didn't care, but Ay did. Ay who never cared whether his son was dead or alive, had gone berserk when he had heard the rumors.

One of the letters that he had written for Merkhet had found its way to Ay, confirming the rumors and sending Ay into a frenzy of anger. Nakhtmin could kill that person who had intercepted the letter and taken it to Ay, but in all probability he was already dead, because Ay wouldn't leave a witness alive.

It was a quiet spring afternoon when Merkhet had come visiting. Nakhtmin had first recited his newest poem to his willing and smitten audience, then after enjoying a goblet of wine, they had closed the door. Merkhet was looking especially handsome that day. The lemon-colored shawl that he wore upon his shoulder threw a glow upon his bronze oiled skin and made it glimmer as he moved.

Nakhtmin too had taken special care with his appearance. He was of a lighter complexion than Merkhet. He was wearing a *shenti* with gold border and he had outlined his blue-green eyes with kohl. He had wanted to please his lover that day, because exactly a year ago, he and Merkhet had first lain together.

That was the day Nakhtmin's dream was destroyed.

They were on his bed, in the throes of passion, both reaching out to touch the rays of that final bliss, when Ay had stormed in.

He had stood there in the middle of his bedchamber, at touching distance from them, sending them scrambling for their *shenties*.

"My son, a *nuk*?" he had shouted. That was just the beginning of a flood of profanities that had continued unabated, until Ay had tired. They had both stood there, their heads bowed in shame.

Then Ay had dismissed Merkhet, and addressed Nakhtmin.

"If only you were on top, I would have forgiven you. Did you learn nothing from the scriptures? Don't you know that receiving a man's seed makes you worse than a woman? Remember how Horus had lost the hand that he had used to capture Seth's seed? What are you willing to lose, *nuk*? Because if I took away the thing you were taking his seed in, you will be dead."

Ay had never called him by his name again, and whenever he had an opportunity he degraded Nakhtmin by calling him a *nuk*.

After that day, he and Merkhet had never met in his house again. Nor in Merkhet's house. He knew that his father would have his friend's house watched. Yet, when they couldn't stay apart, they met in the caves on the cliffs or in the dark alleys of the pleasure houses that dotted the outskirts of Thebes.

He had heard of Merkhet's death six months later. His friend had drowned in the Nile. His heart knew that Ay was behind it.

Nakhtmin never loved again. He never married, for he didn't want to subject a woman to a loveless existence.

But he had a son.

A son given to him by the gods, and taken from him by Ay.

〰 ◊◊◊ 〰

Horemheb touched the bronze cylinder upon his chest

and silently bemoaned the lost glory of Egypt. *What had his beautiful country come to, that its future must be decided by cunning and stealth?*

But deception and treachery were words that were today sequined upon the crown of Egypt – the crown that had last graced the brow of Pharaoh Ay.

When Horemheb was young, he had never expected to witness the trickery and treachery that went on behind the palace walls. He wasn't an ambitious man. He could come up with brilliant military strategies but he lacked the most important quality that a politician must possess.

He didn't have a devious mind.

After his marriage to Mutnedjmet, he had gone back to work. There were rebellions to be quelled, aggressions to be contained, and more than anything, it was important to ensure that Sinai and the land beyond remained in Egypt's control.

So when Pharaoh Amenhotep's son who was later derided throughout Egypt as the Heretic King or Akhenaten the Heretic, ascended the throne of Egypt, Horemheb kept himself busy doing what he did best – keeping the borders of Egypt safe.

The Heretic had abandoned Thebes, the lovely capital of Egypt with its numerous temples and priests, and established a new capital. As the Commander of Egyptian military Horemheb was now required to report to Pharaoh in the new capital.

Horemheb didn't particularly like the new city, especially as both Mutnedjmet and Amenia had decided to stay back in Thebes. This was why he hadn't established his household in the new city of Akhet-aten. He knew that his father-in-law Ay was happy with his decision, for he didn't want Horemheb to become close to the new Pharaoh.

Not that Horemheb was interested in getting close to the Heretic King anyway. He followed the old path and he couldn't imagine how his military campaigns would perform if he didn't have the blessings of *Menthu* and *Neith,* and how he could start his day without offering his prayers to *Horus*.

In the new capital, *Aten* was the only god of consequence. All other gods were banned.

Akhenaten had ruled for thirteen godless years, and Ay had been there with the Heretic King, cheering him on.

Was it any wonder then, that the gods had forsaken the city of Akhet-aten and its inhabitants?

ᗯᗯ 𓊪𓊪𓊪 ᗯᗯ

Ay's body was carefully removed from the bed and placed upon an open reed litter made of densely woven papyrus and edged with gold. All his articles that were made of leather were left behind, for leather was impure and it couldn't accompany the dead.

After Pharaoh Ay's body was removed, the priests, the Grand Vizier, the other important officials, and Nakhtmin, all went inside Pharaoh's office. Before Ay had taken ill, he worked from here, but for the last six months, most of the administrative work had been passed on to Nakhtmin, who had unwillingly accepted the burden, telling himself that he was doing it for *loyalty and friendship*.

It's just a matter of hours now, he thought.

"Where is the Pharaoh's seal ring?" the Head Priest asked, his black beetle eyes reflecting the light of the many lamps that were lit in the room.

Nakhtmin produced a small key from the leather pouch he wore on his belt and went around his father's desk.

They all craned their necks to see what he was doing. That this was all happening in night had imbued everything with an odd spirituality. They said that the *ka* never went too far from the deceased's body and Nakhtmin hoped that the funerary temple was beyond the farthest reaches of Ay's *ka*.

If it were here, it would smite me dead, thought Nakhtmin.

"Here it is," he said glibly as he produced Ay's seal ring from the drawer.

"Why is it here? When it should have been upon Pharaoh's finger?" asked the Grand Vizier, who doubted everything and was suspicious of everyone.

Nakhtmin answered him.

"I removed it from his finger and brought it here after Pharaoh breathed his last. I had to leave his side, and I didn't want the seal ring to be misused."

Everyone nodded. They understood. After all, Ay had himself announced Nakhtmin as the crown prince of Egypt.

He was beyond reproach.

"Ask the goldsmith to step in, so that the deceased Pharaoh's ring may be melted," said the Head Priest. His acolyte shuffled out to fetch the goldsmith, who hurried in with a young servant of his own. The servant carried the crucible and the tiny portable furnace, which would be lighted there, in front of all the dignitaries.

While some may have considered being called for the melting of the seal ring to be an honor, at his hoary old age of seventy, the goldsmith didn't appreciate being dragged out of his bed at this hour of the night.

While the goldsmith busied himself with setting up his equipment for melting the ring, they all sat there. There was nothing to do until the ring had changed into a shapeless glob of gold, ready to be formed into the seal ring of the new Pharaoh.

The priest yawned first. Then the others did.

But Nakhtmin didn't.

Watching the goldsmith, he was transported back to the past – into the time of Queen Tiye, for the goldsmith was also the royal jeweler, and Nakhtmin's dear aunt Queen Tiye, loved her jewels.

And she had given him his son, his dear Prince Tut.

Nakhtmin's mother had died soon after Nakhtmin had turned twenty-two, and for the next ten years, he had been very lonely.

By the age of eighteen, almost all his friends had got married. They went back to their families in the evenings. Even when he met them, Nakhtmin had little to share with them. Their mundane conversations bored the artist in him out of his wits. And the few that led more interesting lives would talk about women or war. Nakhtmin had found relief in poetry and painting, and he would have spent his remaining life confined in his chambers, had Queen Tiye not sent for him.

She had sent for him seventeen years ago.

Seventeen years ago, his son-to-be was six, and he was thirty-two.

Queen Tiye was Pharaoh Amenhotep's wife, Pharaoh Akhenaten's mother, and Pharaoh Tutunkhamun's grandmother, and she was the sweetest soul who ever lived in entire Kemet. Perhaps her only failing was that she was also Ay's sister. And yet, that single failing had brought disaster upon Egypt. Had she not been Ay's sister, or if she hadn't been Amenhotep's wife – Egypt's fortunes wouldn't have dwindled so, for she was the link between Ay and the Egyptian royalty.

Nakhtmin hadn't been close to his aunt when she had been young. It was possible that for a very long time, Queen Tiye must have been quite unaware of her nephew's pitiful existence.

He had first met her when she was in her early sixties. She still had the sweetest smile and the happiest sounding laughter.

When Queen Tiye had learned that he was a scribe and poet, she had called him to her chambers and asked him whether he would be willing to tutor her grandson.

He had heard rumors about the prince. Some said, he looked funny, others had told him that the prince had an odd walk. He hadn't seen the prince until Queen Tiye had introduced him to her.

"Nakht, I want you to tutor our young Prince," Queen Tiye had said, introducing him to the little boy who stood leaning against her chair.

Nakhtmin hadn't noticed the deformities that everyone else had told him about. Instead he had seen a young boy with intelligent eyes, looking at him with hope.

And so, Queen Tiye had given Nakhtmin someone to cherish, once again. Since that day, Nakhtmin had made it his life's mission to teach the boy everything he knew, and he was glad that he did, for when his ward Prince Tut had become Pharaoh Tutankhamun, he had made his teacher proud.

Nakhtmin's memories of the boy king made his eyes sting. If he were alone, he might've blubbered and cried. Here seated among the dozing nobility of Egypt, he had to stop himself from expressing his emotions, but nothing could stop the memories from flooding in.

His walk may have been skewed, but his head worked absolutely fine, Nakhtmin thought.

The boy had been nine when he was made Pharaoh. The cynical ones such as Nakhtmin himself had observed how Ay had maneuvered himself into the position of the Regent. In Akhenaten's lifetime, Ay had been strongly opposed to the idea of Prince Tut becoming Pharaoh.

Queen Tiye had once remarked to Nakhtmin that her brother Ay was more poisonous than the horned viper and the Egyptian asp put together. She had told Nakhtmin that Ay was the man who had poisoned Akhenaten's mind against everyone - the old gods, his wife Nefertiti, his mother Tiye, and even against his little son, the poor boy who bore the curse of royalty and was born with a twisted leg and a cleft palate.

Nakhtmin had found no cause to disagree with the old lady.

When he had first met the young prince, his own heart was full of trepidation. Until then, he had seen Prince Tut only from afar, as a child who didn't run about shouting like other kids of his age did. He walked slowly, and he had heard that special sandals were made for his tiny feet, for they were beginning to curl inward.

His first meeting with the prince would have been a little awkward, had the prince not taken it upon himself to make Nakhtmin comfortable. Prince Tut was sitting upon a low cushioned stool with a sled-table in front of it. Upon it lay papyrus rolls and a set of reed pens.

Nakhtmin had taken his place in front of the prince and introduced himself.

"Yes," the child had replied with more gravity and dignity that Nakhtmin had ever seen displayed in the palace, "*Iry-mut* told me about you. You are the greatest scribe in Egypt. There isn't a hieroglyph that you cannot read. You know five languages and you are the spinner of dreams."

Iry-mut or Guardian Mother was their beloved Queen Tiye. He had never known what Queen Tiye thought about him, but when *Thoth*, the god of learning and truth, spoke in the child's voice, he knew that he had found the essence of his calling.

He would become the spinner of Egypt's dreams.

Nakhtmin had soon realized that the boy was a genius. Elated to be blessed with a pupil so passionate about learning, he poured all that he knew into Prince Tut's willing mind, preparing him to be the future Pharaoh of Egypt, because regardless of Ay's and Pharaoh Akhenaten's disdain for him, the boy still remained the only male heir to the throne of Egypt.

Ay knew this too.

And yet, despite all his shrewdness, Ay was a fool. His foolishness was the product of his own narcissism for he never considered the possibility that he, the most cunning man in Egypt, could ever be wrong. For that reason, he never questioned himself, and his first impressions usually remained his last. This was why Ay had never considered the possibility that little Tut's imperfect body could house a perfectly brilliant mind.

While the child was bright and learned everything quickly, he didn't know of the evil that lurked within the palace walls. Nakhtmin knew about every little thing that went on in the residence of Pharaoh, but the child needed to know only some, and those too after being stripped of their salaciousness.

The young prince's learning went on unhindered, for nobody in the palace was too concerned about what a good-for-nothing scribe was doing with a cursed-by-*Seth* boy, except of course, the boy's *Iry-mut* Queen Tiye, who would always ask about the boy's progress when Nakhtmin went to meet her in the evenings.

Those were the best days of their lives. Nakhtmin's, Prince Tut's, and Queen Tiye's. But this didn't mean that the palace intrigues had stopped too. Ay's devious mind was pulling tricks after tricks.

Until little Tut grows up and becomes Pharaoh, Nakhtmin had thought, *and then Ay will have to stop his shenanigans.*

But then, despite Nakhtmin's prayers and hopes, Ay had begun considering Prince Tut's candidature for becoming his next puppet.

That day Ay had barged into Nakhtmin's chambers unannounced.

"You have been tutoring the boy for a long time now," Ay said, waving him to stay seated. He had been correcting an essay that the young prince had written.

"Yes," he had replied tersely, realizing how quickly Ay was sapping his confidence.

"For three years now, I hear," Ay continued.

"Yes," he answered.

"What do you think of the boy?" he asked. Ay always been direct with him and his mother. Nakhtmin was sure he wasn't so ill tempered around the people that mattered.

Nakhtmin considered the question. He had no concrete idea why Ay wanted his opinion on Prince Tut, but he had some inkling. *I cannot endanger the boy*, he thought frantically, trying to decide what he should tell – *truth or nothing*. He decided upon nothing.

"Nothing," he said.

"Nothing?" Ay asked, his eyebrow quirked.

"There's nothing to tell. He is like any other boy his age," Nakhtmin replied.

"What I mean to ask is," clarified Ay, "Can that dumb calf sit on the throne and keep the crown straight upon his brow?"

The nine-year-old *dumb calf* was sworn in as Pharaoh the next morning.

Nakhtmin knew that Ay was in for a shock. He also knew that his little Pharaoh would need an ally – an honest man, who loved Egypt enough to lay down his life for it.

That man, Nakhtmin remembered, had a square forbidding face and a stout frame.

⸺ 𓏤𓏤𓏤 ⸺

In the shadows of the mountains that fell in the narrow *wadi* between them, Horemheb could see the lights of his camp. He would be there soon. The weight of the bronze cylinder reminded him of his final battle – the one that he still might need to fight.

As the Chief Commander of the Egyptian army and navy, he had fought many battles, and always won them, but in winning them, he had lost more important ones at home.

Horemheb remembered the day he had stopped being a distant spectator and become a player instead.

Had it not been for Nakhtmin, the exquisite young man he had first seen at his wedding with Mutnedjmet, nothing would have changed.

Those were uncertain times. After the heretic king's death, Ay had conspired to put a puppet pharaoh upon the throne and ruled Egypt for a year, after which Ay had announced that the nine-year-old Prince Tut would become the next Pharaoh. Ay himself would be his Regent.

Horemheb was in Akhet-aten at the time of young Tut's coronation, but he hadn't spared the child another thought. Entire Egypt knew that Ay was that accomplished puppeteer who made the pharaohs dance to his tunes, and nobody expected it to be any different with the boy king.

He was to leave the godless city of Akhet-aten the next morning, and he would have, had one of the girls from the harem not accosted him to deliver a scrap of papyrus with a message.

The message was short and unsigned. It said, *"Wait for me in your chamber. I shall come tonight."*

On his way back to the guest-chamber of the royal palace where he used to stay whenever he visited the capital, he had mulled over the message and its mysterious sender. It couldn't be a woman, he thought. He was well past his youth and even in his youth he seldom could set a maiden's heart aflutter. Now, with a face that bore two ungainly battle-scars, it was hard for him to think of a woman falling in love with him so hard that she wanted to meet him in his chambers.

Definitely not a woman, he felt sure.

Horemheb had let out a long sigh and returned to the chambers where he was staying. He had no intention of missing the visit of his mystery caller.

His mysterious visitor had come late in night. With his face and body covered in black, he looked like a thief. Horemheb's military training made his hand respond before his mind did, and before the visitor realized, he had the point of Horem-heb's sword, pushing under his chin.

"Who are you?" Horemheb demanded.

"Put the sword away. I'm here to talk," answered the man in black.

He had withdrawn his sword, and the man had removed his mask.

The face now had the lines of age and the wrinkles of sorrow, but the sparkle in those green-blue eyes was still there – with the light of the lamp reflecting in them, Horemheb saw the sun rise upon the Nile.

"Nakhtmin?" he asked in a shocked voice.

"Shhh," his visitor had brought his finger to his lips and signaled him to stay quiet. "Don't shout."

Horemheb had followed Nakhtmin's advice and clammed up, and Nakhtmin had taken over.

"Egypt needs you here in the capital, and not on the border. The Hittite aren't the ones destroying Egypt," Nakhtmin had said.

"I must follow my orders," Horemheb had tried to counter, but his visitor had shushed him again.

"You must listen to me. This will take time. We might be sitting here all night, talking about it."

And so they had talked - first in the light of a single lamp, then in the dark security of a moonless night. Their whispers kept them connected.

Their conversation hinged upon their common love – Egypt. They both loved their beautiful *Kemet*, and they wanted to save it from being destroyed. That night, Horemheb's suspicions were confirmed.

"We need you here, Horemheb. Prince Tut is now Pharaoh. He is an exceptional boy, astute and observant, and he is already beginning to understand the ill that plagues Egypt," Nakhtmin had explained. "Over the last thirty years, Ay has worked to weaken the royal family's hold over Egypt. First he brainwashed Pharaoh Akhenaten into disowning the old gods and starting a new religion. In doing this, Pharaoh Akhenaten lost the loyalty of his own people. Then by moving the capital here, he lost the most loyal and credible supporters of the crown, for they stayed back in Thebes. Ay and his adopted daughter Nefertiti were the only ones who had remained by Pharaoh Akhenaten's side. They, and more specifically Ay, were the only advisors Pharaoh had. Do you see how my father has been the true ruler of Egypt all these years?"

Horemheb understood. But what he hadn't been able to understand was why Nakhtmin had decided to divulge it all to him, *and why now?*

"Because now that Prince Tut is Pharaoh, things will change. My father thinks of him as a sick child who is wrapped up in his own miseries. I think my father also expects him to die in a few years. When that happens, being the Regent, my father Ay will be quick to declare himself Pharaoh. My father has but one dream. He wants to be the most powerful man in Egypt. He doesn't care for anyone...*anyone at all.* Our young Pharaoh needs an honest ally, and Horemheb, he cannot find a more loyal friend than you."

Horemheb had felt traces of Nakhtmin's pain in his last sentence. He hadn't probed then. It was just their first meeting.

The next morning, Horemheb met Pharaoh Tutankhamun privately. Within moments of their meeting, Horemheb had forgotten the buckteeth, the cleft palate, and the wobbly gait of the child pharaoh. All he remembered was the strange combination of innocence and intelligence. He had never met someone like the child pharaoh before.

Nakhtmin was right. The child had a mind of his own, and before long, he would be taking the reins of Egypt in his own capable hands.

The time of Ay the puppeteer was coming to an end.

In the next ten years, Horemheb had turned into Pharaoh Tutankhamun's closest confidante. He and Nakhtmin too had continued to meet, though infrequently; but Nakhtmin ensured that they never met in the same place twice.

"Why do we have to be so discreet?" he had asked Nakhtmin once.

"Because my father Ay has a hundred eyes and a thousand ears," Nakhtmin said, his voice barely a whisper, like he found it difficult to speak.

And so their clandestine meetings continued. Sometimes Nakhtmin would appear in Horemheb's sleeping chambers in the middle of the night, and wake him up and talk to him.

Horemheb had once bantered light-heartedly with his nocturnal visitor.

"Can we not meet somewhere else? These nightly visits, if discovered, might be construed differently," he had jested.

Nakhtmin had laughed. His laughter was laced with bitterness.

"My father often calls me a *nuk*. So if we are discovered, an amorous relationship between us may appear to be entirely plausible, especially to my father. The men of military, on the other hand, are known to keep themselves supplied with young boys. Aren't they?" he had asked him.

"Not me," Horemheb had replied. But he was reminded of his own Commander from his youth.

"Yes, I know," Nakhtmin had said, his voice shaking a little. "You are a man of conviction and character, and Egypt needs someone like you guiding it to its destiny."

The mark that Ay had left on his soul was indelible.

〰 ۝۝۝ 〰

After the ring was melted and the nobles and the

priests had left Pharaoh's office, Nakhtmin had returned to his chambers. Ay's death had left him spent physically but charged mentally. He knew he wouldn't sleep a wink tonight.

He lay upon his bed, his eyes riveted to the ceiling upon which he himself had painted the life of the boy king Tutankhamun, the child who he had loved as his son.

His life would have been short, even if it hadn't been cut shorter. The young pharaoh had planned everything. He had the perspicacity to choose Horemheb as his successor, and he had signed a will to that effect.

Nakhtmin's memories of that day were as clear as the summer sky – not a speck of doubt clouded anything. That was the day Pharaoh Tutankhamun had died.

Except that Tutankhamun hadn't died, he had been murdered.

A month earlier, he had announced Horemheb as his successor. Pharaoh Tutankhamun, then nineteen and no longer a young boy but an able administrator, had announced that if he died childless, Horemheb would succeed him. Pharaoh had made the announcement in front of the court officials and the priests.

To Nakhtmin's surprise, Ay had smiled the whole time and even suggested to the young king that they should make a will. And so a will was made. Unfortunately, Ay who had pioneered this idea had been given the responsibility of being the executioner of the will.

The day after the will was made and locked away, Horemheb had gone north to lead a military campaign in Asia. Ay had continued being the Regent, which gave him unlimited access to Pharaoh. Nakhtmin had once again disappeared into his chambers, where he wrote poetry and painted his walls.

That fateful evening, Nakhtmin had gone to meet Pharaoh. The pharaoh's chambers for Tutankhamun had been moved to ground level. His left foot had now begun to turn inward so much that despite his cane, he couldn't walk without experiencing pain, and climbing stairs alone was simply impossible for him.

This was why, when Nakhtmin didn't find Pharaoh in his chambers, he had felt afraid.

"Where's Pharaoh?" he had shouted at a chambermaid who was trying to scuttle past him.

"Upstairs with *Iry-pat*," she had stammered, pointing a finger to the staircase that went up all the way to the terrace, from where one could look down into the central court of the palace.

He was about to rush upstairs, when he saw a flash of color out of the corner of his eye. He looked up. Near the parapet wall that went around the terrace, he saw them. And then he saw Pharaoh fall.

Nobody else saw what happened, for the angle was such that only someone standing on the first few steps of the staircase could see what had happened, and Ay hadn't expected anyone to be there.

Nakhtmin had screamed, and Ay had seen him.

But how could he control his emotions when his only child was lying in a crumpled heap?

His little prince was dead.

Killed.

Later that evening, Ay had summoned him to his room.

"What did you see?" Ay had asked Nakhtmin.

"You killed him," distraught, he had accused Ay. That had been his mistake. He should have done something else. Anything but that, for by doing so, he had alerted Ay.

Ay had calmly walked to his desk where a wooden box lay. He opened the lid and withdrew a bundle of letters. He had recognized them, even after all those years. They were the letters that he had written to Merket.

"*Nuk*, don't push me to leak the content of these letters. Egypt will shun you, if I did. Forget what you saw. Go back to your room and paint a picture of your beautiful Pharaoh Tut, but don't do anything to upset my plan."

Nakhtmin hadn't forgotten, but he hadn't done the right thing either.

He had known that Tutankhamun had wanted Ay to be his successor, but he had not tried to reach him.

He was afraid of Ay.

But Nakhtmin hadn't forgotten. He had carried both Merkhet and young Tut in his heart.

After Ay had quickly buried Pharaoh Tutankhamun and wedded his widow Ankhesenamun to lay his claim upon the throne, Nakhtmin had made a promise to Horemheb and to his dead boy-king.

He would bring back the days of Egypt's lost glory.

He would become the Spinner of Egypt's dreams.

Today, looking at the bundle of his letters upon his desk, he realized that soon his heart would feel a lot lighter.

Soon.

ᴧᴧᴧ 𓏤𓏤𓏤 ᴧᴧᴧ

When Horemheb reached his camp, the sky was beginning to brighten and the stars could no longer be seen. Lord Tepi, his second-in-command, greeted him with a smile. Tepi covered his worried look with feigned anger, the moment he saw his friend and superior.

"What took you so long?" he had asked him with concern. "I was about to set out with a search party."

"Do you expect the Commander of the Egyptian army to be gobbled up by the desert?" he asked, while taking him by his arm and steering him into his tent. The guards straightened their spears allowing them to pass. Inside the tent was lit with two lamps, one of which stood upon his wood-table. They were on their way to contain a new surge in the Hittite aggression on Egypt's northern border, and Horemheb seldom required anything more than a straw-bed to bunk.

"You must be careful," Tepi continued his banter, "now you don't have Amenhotep the Magnificent saving your cheeky behind."

Horemheb ignored his insinuation and took the metal cylinder off his neck.

"What is in it?" Tepi asked, snatching the cylinder away from him.

"A scroll," replied Horemheb, falling upon the straw mattress that was spread on the ground.

"What scroll?" Tepi asked.

From where Horemheb lay, he could see the Pharaoh's seal.

"I think I know what it might be. But the seal must be broken only in the court at Thebes," Horemheb replied and closed his eyes.

Tepi too thought he knew what it contained.

"For Egypt," he said, touching the cylinder with a reverential awe.

For our Egypt, thought the Commander of the Egyptian military.

᙮᙮᙮ ◊◊◊ ᙮᙮᙮

The night had ended and a new day had dawned. Nakhtmin had not slept a wink. He could sleep later, but right now he needed to finish what he had started.

It was time for him to exact his final revenge.

For the last whole year, he had transformed into Ay's

197

vision of an ideal son, and he had finally corrected the wrong. It was only a matter of hours before the next Pharaoh of Egypt would be anointed.

His brilliant father had played into the hands of a *nuk* who he had detested all his life. Lying in his bed, counting his remaining days and memorizing the verses from the Book of the Dead, Ay had called him to his side.

"Son," he said.

Nuk was what Nakhtmin heard.

"Son, you are a scribe. Go into my office and get a scroll and some pens, and then write down what I say."

Nakhtmin had complied.

He was writing down what Ay was dictating, until he realized that it was a will. Ay was leaving the crown of Egypt to him, Nakhtmin.

"Why father?" he had asked.

He had never questioned his father. Perhaps his question had surprised Ay as much as the will had surprised Nakhtmin, for he was hit by a long bout of cough that made Nakhtmin run for the spittoon and hold it in front of his father's mouth. He threw a large ball of phlegm into it, and sank back into his pillows.

I'm helping a monster. I'm nursing the man who tortured my mother, murdered my love, killed my young friend and Pharaoh, and turned my own life into a putrid stinking mess!

He shrugged, letting the debilitating thought drop away.

"Why?" he had asked again.

"Because you are the only one. I have nobody else to bequeath it to. I worked so hard to get here, and now, I have nobody to inherit it. You don't deserve it, but you are the best I've got. When I leave the world and move to afterlife, I want my name being carried on. You will promise that you will rule as Ay the Second."

Then he coughed again, slightly, and continued.

"And also because you kept my secret."

Nakhtmin was reminded of Tutankhamun's death. He had seen the fall, and what had caused it. He should have spoken, but his silence had saved his life.

I kept quiet, because I was a coward, he thought miserably.

Aloud he said, "I did so, because you threatened me." His voice trembled with his bottled up anger.

"You had your reasons," replied Ay.

And so Nakhtmin had got his answer and he had seen the path of his redemption marked clear and strong.

He knew that all his father would see in the scroll would be blurred ink. All he had to do was change the text of the will, and things will be as Tutankhamun had wanted them to be.

"Make two copies of it, Nakhtmin, and then bring them to me so that I can put my stamp on them in front of the priests and the officials. Do you remember what had happened when that sick boy had died? I suspect that Horemheb will try to pull the same trick on you. He does have a stronger claim than you through my daughter Mutnedjmet. Keep a copy with you and another in my office drawer – put them in two gold cylinders and then stamp them with my seal."

A man as self-centered as Ay could never expect anyone to do what Nakhtmin had done. He couldn't imagine that what had meant the world to him, meant so little to his son.

Nakhtmin raised himself from his bed and picked the bundle of the letters.

First, he would burn them.

Then he would burn Ay's soul.

Ay's sarcophagus would be sealed in his tomb, but his *ka* would never find his body.

〰 𓂀𓂀 〰

Horemheb's camp was buzzing with activity that morning. The runner from the palace had arrived early. He came on a horse draped in black, with a black flag fluttering behind him.

"My Lord, the past night, Pharaoh Kheperkheperure Ay It-netjer began his journey to the afterlife. *Iry-pat* Nakhtmin desires your presence at the palace immediately," he had bowed in front of Horemheb, and announced heartily.

Nobody mourns the heartless one, thought Horemheb as he dismissed the boy.

The bronze cylinder that contained Pharaoh's last will, lay upon his table and under his crocodile-skin armor. He had to take it along. Nakhtmin had reminded him twice.

"The will is important, and you must bring it to the court tomorrow. My father had sealed it in front of the priests, and they will ask for it," he had told Horemheb.

〰〰 𓏤𓏤𓏤 〰〰

Several weeks later, after all the funerary rituals for Ay were completed, and his red quartzite sarcophagus was, with all ceremony, sealed in his tomb, Horemheb and Nakhtmin sat playing a game of *senet.*

Horemheb had lost yet another game. Nakhtmin was a far better player than he was.

"It's just a game," Horemheb said, pushing the *senet*-board away.

"Yes, Your Majesty," agreed Nakhtmin.

They were sitting in Pharaoh Horemheb's antechamber. Pharaoh Ay's recently widowed wife Ankhesenamun and Horemheb's wives Amenia and Mutnedjmet lay upon a couch and watched them play.

"I am terribly pleased that I don't have to marry again," Ankhesenamun remarked.

Nakhtmin heard her and chuckled. "Horemheb has no need to marry you, Ankhesenamun. Mutnedjmet is our late Pharaoh's daughter, and with her as his wife, Horemheb has a stronger claim on the throne than anyone else alive today."

"And we have two copies of Ay's will," Horemheb added.

They laughed. It was refreshing to hear their laughter, thought Horemheb.

"Majesty, I'll let you win this game on one condition," Nakhtmin addressed his friend, popping a fig in his mouth.

"Anything for you, my friend," Horemheb replied, looking at him fondly.

"Erase my father's name and deeds from history."

Horemheb stared at the board for a long time, then looked up and smiled at Nakhtmin.

"Since there appears to be no other way to win this game, Nakht, I will do what you ask of me."

Nakhtmin smiled and moved his piece away in the wrong direction, letting Horemheb win the game.

"Thank you for letting me win, my friend," said Horemheb. "But why do you want to erase your father from history?" he asked, lowering his voice, so that the women couldn't hear him.

Nakhtmin shook his head.

"Because I don't want the walls of Egypt stained with his misdeeds, and also because in his afterlife, I don't want him to find his way back to our dear Kemet," he said.

"But the gods judge us," countered Horemheb, "*Anubis* would have…"

"*Anubis* would have weighed his heart. But Horemheb, the man had no heart, and if he had one, regret never weighed it down. What if it had weighed less then *Ma'at*'s feather? If it had, after plunging Egypt in darkness and despair, and after killing our dear Pharaoh Tutankhamun, the man would have spent his afterlife in heaven. I couldn't take that chance, could I?"

Nakhtmin paused, and then added, "Horemheb, I can spin dreams in prose and poetry, I can also paint them on papyrus – but to make those dreams come true, Egypt needs you, and this is why I let you win. I am a scribe, a poet, and a painter, not an administrator or a soldier. I would have been a terrible Pharaoh. With you as Pharaoh, I know that my Egypt and my happiness are both safe."

〰 ۝ 〰

The skiff bobbed softly upon the bosom of Nile. The late evening breeze that blew upon the calm waters of the river was beginning to cool down. Nakhtmin had rowed the skiff away from the palace, close to the west bank.

Ankhesenamun sat opposite to him. Ay's death had been good to her. She didn't look skeletal anymore. She had lost the hollows in her cheeks and under her eyes. She had outlined her eyes with galena and the green malachite was almost the same color as Nile and she wore a long white linen skirt. If he had his paints with him, Nakhtmin would have loved to paint her, the way she looked now.

"So where is he actually buried?" she asked him, jettisoning him out of his dream, throwing him face down upon the burning sand of the land beyond the cliffs.

"Beyond the cliff," he replied.

Beyond the cliff, under the sand, the way the poorest Egyptian was buried, except that no Egyptian was ever buried without his heart. The heart was where Nile lived. It was where life dwelled. The heart was what *Anubis* demanded when one died and reached *Duat*. Ay was buried without his heart, and without his organs – for his organs were in his tomb. They had to put them there, or the priests may have asked questions.

"Do you think, his *ka* would ever find him again?" she asked him.

He thought about it for a moment then replied.

"No. It won't, and even if it did, Ay would never rise again."

They sat together, quietly listening to the sounds of flapping wings and splashing water. The birds were going home, and it was time for them to leave too. Ankhesenamun and Nakhtmin shared a close bond – a bond that only they understood. That bond had brought them closer than they would be if they had decades of marriage between them. Their lives had been destroyed by the same man. Sitting there in that tiny skiff, they felt at peace for the first time in their lives.

"I shall not grudge another marriage, Nakht," she said, her eyes reading his.

He looked back, his heart aching to give her the comfort she desired. But he knew he couldn't. He couldn't even tell her why. She kept looking into his eyes, searching for an answer. When she found none, she simply pressed his knee and removed her hand.

"And I shall not grudge your refusal. I will only ask you to be my friend forever."

That she understood his inability to answer and didn't attempt to pry loose his reason, made him choke. He wasn't good at handling tears the way other men were.

I cannot cry, he told himself.

"You can cry, if it helps. He is gone…forever! He can never return to torture us, Nakht. Spin your dreams, weave them into your life, because you have saved us and saved Egypt," she said.

Her words broke the dam that Ay had built around his tears. They gushed out, breaking the barriers, sweeping the debris of nightmares that had settled deep into his memories. Washing away his pain, they cleansed his soul - healing and closing the wounds, they rolled down his cheeks and fell upon the trembling knuckles of his hands that held the oars.

ᴡᴡ 𝇋𝇋𝇋 ᴡᴡ

Historical Notes:

Amenhotep III, also known as Amenhotep the Magnificent, was the father of Akhenaten. Amenhotep's chief royal wife was Queen Tiye.

Akhenaten, the Heretic King who started a monotheistic religion to replace the many gods of Egypt, and moved the capital of Egypt from Thebes to Akhet-aten, was earlier known as Amenhotep IV, and was the son of Amenhotep III and Queen Tiye.

Horemheb had begun his career as a soldier in Amenhotep III's army. His first wife was Amenia. According to historians, his second wife Mutnedjmet was Ay's daughter.

Ay was Queen Tiye's brother and possibly the father of Queen Nefertiti who was the wife of Pharaoh Akhenaten.

Pharaoh Tutankhamun, known as the boy king, was born Tutankhaten. The scan of his mummy has revealed that his left foot was severely twisted inward and he must have experienced a lot of pain in walking. Walking sticks have also been discovered in his tomb. His mummy has a fractured skull, which has been attributed by some historians to a fall.

Tutankhamun ascended the throne as a nine-year-old child. Ay was his Regent during his reign. Tutankhamun moved the capital back to Thebes, and reinstated the old gods.

Tutankhamun had declared that in the event of his dying childless, Horemheb, who was the Commander of the Egyptian military and the Fan Bearer on the right side of the Pharaoh, would succeed him as Pharaoh.

Tutankhamun and his wife Ankhesenamun had two stillborn children. At the age of nineteen, Tutankhamun who was still childless died of an unknown cause.

Ay ascended the throne after Tutankhamun's death. Some historians claim that Ay killed Tutankhamun. He ruled for three years.

Before his death, Ay had announced that his son Nakhtmin would be the next pharaoh.

History is not clear about why Nakhtmin did not become Pharaoh. Instead, Horemheb succeeded Ay. Horemheb systematically set about destroying everything related to the Amarna period.

Amarna period refers to the time in Ancient Egyptian history, when the capital of Egypt was moved to Akhet-aten.

Ay's tomb was found in the Valley of Kings. It had a red quartzite sarcophagus that contained no mummy.

Nuk was the Ancient Egyptian term used to describe a man who took to lower position when two men engaged in sex. It was considered to be a term of gross insult.

Story Five

THE BLUE LILY

~ | Old Kingdom – First Dynasty | ~

THE BLUE LILY

The air was rife with the smell of fear. It escaped from their pores and filled the space as they sat there waiting for the bell to ring. The bell would ring, they never doubted it – the only question was, when. They hoped that it wouldn't ring tonight. They wanted to live another night – a night soaked in fear and in the murky anticipation of the dark future that awaited them. They wanted to live – all seven of them.

They knew that outside their dormitory, within the palace walls, there were others who felt the same fear tonight. They were the women of the harem, maids and servant boys, and guards. Their names, unlike those of the chosen seven, would be determined through a lottery overseen by the priests of *Anubis*.

Quite like the seven chosen, they were waiting and hoping that gods would intervene.

Quite like the seven chosen, they knew that the gods hadn't listened to their prayers when the previous King had died.

When the bell would ring for the seven of them, and

for many others, it would announce not just the death of their King, but their deaths as well.

〰 𝕼𝕼𝕼 〰

Mentu sat on his cot, shivering. The evening air that blew in from the window in his modest room was balmy and it gave him no cause to shiver, but he shivered nonetheless.

His concubine Khuit sat beside him, her fingers knit into his. She wasn't slated to die, the way Mentu was, but she felt the tension nonetheless.

Khuit felt uncomfortable in the silence that stretched between them, but she had no words for the situation tonight. It was only a matter of time. The King had lived for more than sixty years and ruled for forty-five, and for most of his sixty years he had been almost as wide as he was tall. He had been walking with a stick for the last ten years, and he couldn't sit down nor stand up without his buttocks purring and prattling. But this wasn't the worse of it all. For the last many years, the King had been experiencing trouble breathing, and two days ago, he had gone into convulsions. The royal physician had given his verdict. The King's heart, the seat of life in his body, was not functioning correctly – and so they all knew that the end was near and more a matter of when than if.

"It can happen anytime," Mentu noted absently.

Khuit nodded. She had been living with Mentu for the last ten years, but she had never seen him so distraught before. He hadn't eaten since morning.

"Will you be able to handle it?" Mentu asked, pressing Khuit's hand. He had asked the question twice before and each time Khuit had nodded. She nodded again.

"Say it," he insisted. He wanted to hear the sound of

her voice and feel the conviction he hoped it would carry. Khuit was a talkative woman who seldom ran out of things to say, but in the last two days, she had barely spoken.

"Yes," she replied laconically. He attributed their lack of communication to their situation. *After all, how often was loyalty rewarded by death?*

"When the bell rings, I must go out and join the others," he said. In absence of any other sound, his own voice provided him some solace.

"Yes," she whispered. Then she wrapped her arms around him and whispered in his ears. "Don't think about it. Put your feelings aside and accept everything."

Accept everything? Accept that for being the best royal cook, he was rewarded with death? Accept that for serving the King loyally for more than three decades, he would be made to follow the King into the afterlife? But then Mentu had stepped into the job with a clear understanding of the repercussions. It was a different matter that thirty years ago, when King was himself a young man full of life, Mentu had neglected to appreciate the full consequences of his job.

"I must prepare myself," he muttered extricating his hand from her grip. His palm felt clammy, almost wet with perspiration.

"Have you kept the will in a secure place?" he asked, once again, mainly to make small talk and fill the empty air with sound.

"Yes," she replied.

"Remember that the will can be executed only after the burial," he reminded her.

"Yes, I know," she acknowledged.

"This had to happen one day," he said, consoling himself more than her. He had a feeling that she was a lot more courageous than he was and it didn't surprise him. She had spent many years of her life on the wharves and quays, doing odd jobs at the eateries and lodges, and filling the gaps by prostituting herself to the sailors and the soldiers. He had met her ten years ago, and fallen in love with her. Since he met her, Mentu had become estranged from his wife and children. They lived in Thinis and he in Abdju, from where the King ruled Egypt. In Abdju, he shared his living quarters with Khuit.

Something tinkled outside. He tensed.

"It's not the bell," Khuit said.

"No, it isn't the bell," he agreed. It was the sound of a bracelet or an anklet, perhaps a slave-girl in the courtyard outside. Tonight, everyone was awake – not just the seven chosen ones, or those who still waited to learn whether they had to follow their Pharaoh into the afterlife, but almost everyone else too.

And then suddenly, without warning, the bell rang.

It sounded coarse and ugly, like the gong had grown thorns of metal, which were scrapping against the inner surface of the bell, making it bleed and screech in pain.

The bell rang seven times then stopped.

The King was dead.

Wails arose in the palace and in the servant-quarters alike.

Mentu felt a cold sheet of fear cascade down upon him. He didn't want to die, but now death was inevitable. Not merely inevitable it was now imminent. In a few hours, they will all be dead. They would follow Pharaoh out of this world and into the next.

He didn't want to leave this world. He wanted to live.

He turned to Khuit, took her in his arms, and kissed her wildly. Then his arms fell to his sides and he let her go. There no point prolonging the agony. Suddenly, he wanted to be in the Great Hall, with all those others whose lives were inextricably linked to their king's – and whose lives were now about to end.

Never before had he felt such closeness with any of

them, but right now, all he wanted was to be with them – for only they knew what he was feeling. Nobody else could even remotely understand his pain. Not even Khuit, for Khuit wasn't dying. She wasn't staring into the deep dark abyss that had opened right under his feet.

"Let us go," he said. His own voice sounded alien to him.

"Give me a moment," she replied and got up.

He didn't want her to go anywhere. Absently, he wondered why she would want to separate from him at the most tragic moment of his life.

"Khuit," he reached out and held her wrist. "Don't go. I'm very nervous. Let us go to the Great Hall together."

Khuit bent down and kissed his forehead. Then she disengaged her hand.

"Don't be anxious. I'll be back in a moment," she comforted him, and left through the door that went into the little chamber where she kept her *ankh*-table.

He sat there waiting, his mind blank and his heart racing.
He wanted to live…with Khuit.

Mentu found it difficult to keep sitting and waiting.
What was she doing?

He rose and crossed the room to enter the *ankh*-chamber.

She sat there at her ankh-table smiling coquettishly at her reflection in the mirror.

"Khuit," he had croaked, confused and afraid.

Her expression had changed so quickly that he wondered if he had ever seen that smile on her face.

"Oh Mentu, I was just preparing myself for everything," she pointed to the scarab pendant that lay upon her table. "I know that you are afraid of things going wrong, but I am not. I am sure that everything will be fine. Just give me another moment," she planted a kiss on his lips and smiled at him.

Mentu smiled at her tenderly. She was right.

Fear killed one's ability to reason.

He left her and went back to the bedchamber. A small chest of drawers stood in a corner. He pulled the top-drawer open and removed a vial no bigger than his little finger.

He was glad that he hadn't scrimped and bought the full vial.

〰 ◊◊◊ 〰

He opened his eyes or he thought he had, for he could see nothing. He blinked. Nothing changed. Mentu blinked again, wondering if his eyes were really open. They were, for he could feel them opening and shutting, but he saw nothing – just an even spread of black. It was pitch dark in the place he was, and he had no idea where he could be.

Another thought, more enervating than before, occurred to him.

Was he alive or had he already transcended the plane of living and entered Duat?

He tried to look around in the darkness, hoping to make out the shapes that surrounded him.

Could he see the jackal-headed god Anubis holding the scales upon which his heart would be weighed?

He strained to hear the sounds.

Could he hear the sound of water splashing and the roar of Ammit, the divine devourer of the evil hearts, who had the face of a crocodile and the body of a hippopotamus?

He sniffed the air.

Did it smell any different? Did it smell like the wet fur of a dog or the fart of a hippopotamus?

He saw nothing but he heard the flapping of a bird's wings and he smelled guano. Mentu tried hard to remember the description of the afterlife, but he failed to recall birds. The feather of *Ma'at* against which his heart would be weighed had no reason to be covered with guano and he didn't expect either *Thoth* or *Anubis* to have grown wings only to confuse him.

He felt sure that he was someplace else, definitely on earth and still alive, but wherever he was, he was finding it difficult to breathe.

Mentu tried moving his hands and his feet but failed. His feet were bound together, the same as his hands. His bounds cut into his skin when he tried stretching and breaking them. It was clear that he was bound and thrown into a dark place, possibly in a cave. But he couldn't determine why he was short of breath.

He tried to straighten his legs, but he couldn't. There was no space. His unshod feet felt a knot of coarse linen. He tried to push his feet against it, but the knot resisted and he felt linen straining all around him. And then the realization hit him like a bolt from the sky.

He was bound and packed inside a sack made of coarse linen. His knees were bent and his hands were tied together...*in the front.* The people, who had done this to him, obviously didn't expect him to attempt an escape.

He realized that he was going to die, and for a moment he wondered whether being buried with his king would have been a better option. He would at least have woken up in *Duat* where he would answer for his king, and his king would speak well of him.

Overcome with a frustration too deep and dark, he screamed. His scream echoed and rebounded to him again and again, fading away slightly each time. He listened to the echoes until they died. Then he screamed again.

After he had drained himself, he fell into an exhausted sleep. His body crammed into the linen sack, his hands and feet tied, he slept and dreamed.

He remembered Khuit as he had first met her. Her eyes beaming with innocence, untouched by the pain of her profession, she looked at him with love. Then her soft gaze slowly transformed into the harsh glare of a vulture's eye – and she looked upon him the way the vulture looked upon a dying man – with brazen impatience. He heard the flapping of the wings again, and saw Khuit swoop down upon him, the vast bright blue sky behind her. Then, suddenly her expression changed - it mellowed down. She covered his face with her wings, and told him that she would protect him – that she had a plan. And then he saw himself preparing his will.

Fitfully, he watched Khuit, the vulture, swoop down upon him, wresting the scroll of his will from him with its beak and leaving him for dead.

The flapping of the wings filled the empty air again.

But now he heard a new sound - a series of squeaks that belonged to a rat.

He felt his teeth with his tongue. They hadn't gagged him. His friend, the rat, had squeaked to give him an invaluable lesson.

"Use your teeth, you fool!" He chided himself.

〰〰 ◊◊◊ 〰〰

It was the morning after the King's death and Khuit hadn't slept a wink the whole night.

King Djer, son of King Hor-Aha and Queen Khenthap, was dead. His body had been taken away for embalming, and so were the bodies of his lesser wives, concubines, dwarves, servants, and dogs.

They had all died to keep him company.

First, there were the seven chosen ones including

216

Mentu - they had known all along that they would be buried with the king. Then there were the ones whose names went into the draw. Through the lottery, five hundred and seventy three men and women and sixteen dogs, had been chosen to accompany the King into the afterlife.

As was the royal decree, everyone was first given the ritual bath, and then they were given fresh perfumed clothes to wear. The bath and the change of clothes had another purpose to fulfill – they ensured that nobody could carry a weapon inside. Later, after they were served dinner and wine, they were served a concoction made of poppy flower. It lowered their defenses and made them more tractable, for then they were made to consume poison.

Khuit remembered everything with numbing clarity.

Trouble had begun when the bell had rung last night.

Before the bell was sounded, most of the King's chosen companions for the afterlife had hung from a thread of hope. They prayed for their King to get well, and their prayers were as heartfelt as they could ever be, for if the King lived, they would live too. Only when the sound of the bell pierced through the heavy air, and sliced their hearts, they lost all hope.

In the time before the Kings, it was said that heartfelt prayers said with hope could make the dead rise and walk. But with the ringing of the bell, hope had died, and so those who had been selected to die had screamed and cried. They hugged their loved ones and tried to cling on to them – they all had to be dragged to ceremony, where depending upon who they were, they sat in different tiers.

The ceremony, ironically called the *Awakening*, was held in the Great Hall, where upon a dais, the body of the King was placed. Closest to the King's body, sat the queens, the concubines, and the maids. Other than the King's Royal Consort's, everyone else's name had gone into the lottery. Many of those selected had to be dragged out into the hall – a few had to be chained, but eventually they were all in the Great Hall.

The servants were talking about the King's newest concubine, a young woman of nineteen, who had tried to hide herself in one of the reed baskets containing dirty kitchen linen, so that she may not be found in time for the *Awakening*. Unfortunately for her, the launderers had arrived early and discovered her hiding within the basket.

Another unfortunate soul, a guard, had tried to escape by scaling the walls of the palace, but he was caught and brought back.

Last night, Khuit too had been there in the Great Hall. They allowed a member of the family to be present at the *Awakening*, and the chosen one could give the name of the person they wanted to share their last meal with. Mentu had given her name, and so she was there with him.

In the first tier, closest to the center where the King's body lay, sat the women from the harem.

Khuit had remembered the tragic faces of those women. She had found it difficult to imagine what the women must be feeling as they sat there, anxious and fearful. Most of the King's lesser wives and concubines were young and beautiful, and they were dying for a sixty-year-old man to whom they meant nothing.

She had felt odd, almost guilty, to be sitting in the same hall as those women.

She had tried alleviating her guilt.

In their eyes and everyone else's, I am losing something very dear to me. I'm losing Mentu, and unlike them, Mentu was selected to die when he had been promoted to the position of the Chief Royal Cook. Unlike them, I've lived with this sword hanging upon my neck all these years, she had told herself.

In the second tier of those condemned to die, behind the women of the harem, sat the dwarves and the royal servants, and the seven chosen ones, including Mentu.

Mentu had tried to inform his son about his impending death, but he had no idea whether or not the message had reached him. It wasn't important, for the King's officials would ensure that Mentu's family would be taken care of. His son might even be given a job at the palace, which Mentu hoped would not happen. He didn't want his son to die the way he was dying.

Khuit knew that she had no reason to foster a grudge against Mentu's family, and yet, deep down in her heart, she hated it when he spoke of his son with such fondness. In her opinion, his wife was a middle-aged cow who couldn't keep her husband, and his son was a good-for-nothing brat who excelled at siphoning off his father's wealth.

In the third tier sat the men of the King's personal guard. There were twenty of them. Young and strong, they were all dying so that they may continue to protect the diseased old man in his afterlife.

Khuit wasn't a religious person. She knew the names of only a handful of gods and goddesses and she could hardly remember any of the hymns and prayers. She had lived her life, a day at a time, and she hadn't regretted a single moment of it. *At least not until the time she had started living with Mentu.*

In the final tier stood the King's dogs, tethered to their posts. Khuit looked at them and thought that the dogs were the luckiest among the condemned for they didn't know what was coming.

The fear of looking death in the eye knowing that there's no escape is terrible enough, but knowing that your death is untimely and purposeless is even worse, thought Khuit.

"Khuit," Mentu had said, his food untouched. "I don't want to eat."

She looked around. Nobody was eating, except the dogs.

"Don't eat," she whispered in his ear. "It's only a matter of time. Everything will be fine."

"Will it be?" he asked. The question was rhetorical. He only wished to quell his fear.

"Drink the poppy juice," she told him, as the boy with the poppy juice portions found his way to them.

"I'll lose consciousness…and my will to fight back," Mentu whined. He didn't want to lose consciousness. He knew what would happen next. Once he had consumed the juice, his consciousness and his will to resist would dim along with his ability to feel pain.

Once they had all lost their ability to struggle and fight back, they would be killed…*sacrificed.*

"I will be here," Khuit had comforted him.

"So you would be. But what if something goes wrong?" he asked.

"Nothing will," Khuit wrapped her arms around him as the boy approached them and handed her a portion of poppy juice.

Mentu had been a brat.
He had persistently refused to drink the juice.

ᨆᨆ 𓈖𓈖 ᨆᨆ

Upon the dirt floor of a deep vertical shaft, somewhere on the outskirts of Egypt's capital Abdju, a sack of linen shook slightly.

Mentu's consciousness had still not recovered from the combined effect of the poppy juice, the poison, and its antidote. His memories, his dreams, and his reality were all jostling with one another to occupy his thoughts.

His memories too were a strange combination of new and old.

"A few more minutes," he had pleaded with her at the

Awakening, when she had tried to make him drink the poppy juice. Mentu had tried to avoid drinking it for the juice would make him lose his ability to see things clearly.

But when one of the guards had surreptitiously pushed the tip of his dagger under his chin, he had capitulated.

The juice had begun to influence his senses almost immediately. It was an odd feeling, but he felt time slowing down. Voices were turning into drawls and everything that moved, moved very slowly. He saw details that he hadn't seen before. He saw the beauty of the colors worn by the King's wives and concubines. He realized that the food that was in his plate had beautiful texture and it smelled divine. He looked at Khuit and realized that her eyes were clear and dry, and that she looked beautiful and young, and then his gaze dropped to her lips. He saw that they were trembling.

He knew that something wasn't right!

The *Awakening* had begun three hours after the bell had tolled. Sitting there in the Great Hall with the juice of poppy splashing inside him, his worst fear was confirmed.

Around her beautiful long neck, Khuit wore the blue lily pendant that she hadn't worn once in the last ten years. Set in gold, it had three blue petals of turquoise and a green sepal of beautiful olive peridot. For hundreds of years, the wharf wenches of the delta had worn that pendant. The blue lily was a symbol of intoxication and passion – the two feelings that entwined to make the rope that bound men to the wenches and the love-priestesses. It was the amulet of their calling.

But her beautiful blue lily pendant had no chamber for the anti-dote.

The scarab pendant was the one with the hidden chamber – and she had left it lying on her *ankh*-table. She couldn't have forgotten it. Not when she knew that without the antidote, he would be dead – and not when she had herself pointed it out to him moments before they had left for the *Awakening*.

The gods had wanted him to live – or why else would he have chanced upon her when she was smiling at her reflection? Why would he have otherwise flushed his system with the remaining antidote in the vial, just before he had left for the *Awakening?*

The antidote had cost him a fortune and about six months to procure. The man who had traveled all the way from Nubia to deliver it to him had told him that the antidote would remain effective for six to eight hours after being consumed. Even six hours would have been sufficient time for him to attempt an escape, but the poppy juice had put him to sleep.

Their initial plan required that he drank the poppy juice and then imbibed the poison. Khuit was then to pass the antidote to him.

Except that she hadn't brought it with her.

Suddenly he was thirsty. His thirst jettisoned him out of his reverie, and brought his consciousness back to his present situation.

Mentu's mouth felt dry, but he knew he wouldn't die of thirst. If his intuition was right, not more than a whole day had passed since the ceremony, and from what he had heard, humans could live for days without water.

Don't panic, he reprimanded himself.

Mentu brought up his bound hands to the small hole that he had made in the sack by chewing it through. He pondered upon the problem. The hole was still small, but if he could hook his finger or his thumb into it, he might be able to tear it and make it bigger.

Worth a try, he thought, and wiggled the thumb of his right hand into the hole.

The material was strong, but his saliva had weakened the yarn, so after a few tugs, it gave way. He fit his face into the hole, gasping and gulping, sucking in as much air as he could. As the air rushed in, he felt rejuvenated. The mist that was swirling upon his thoughts began to settle down, and he found himself thinking more clearly.

It took him a few minutes to become aware of the musty feel of the air. The smell of guano had turned stronger, and it made his stomach churn. Grateful that his stomach was empty, he considered his options. His hands and legs were still tied, and he was lying on the damp dirt floor of a cave or a vertical shaft. It was clear that he wasn't buried in the king's tomb for he knew that its floor and the walls were made of mud-brick.

Where exactly am I? he wondered.

He turned so that he was now lying on his back and looking up. Stars twinkled in a tiny hole above him.

"If I am not dead, then what I see above is the sky, and I am inside a vertical shaft somewhere," he murmured. The sound of his own voice surprised him. It made him feel more alive.

"How do I untie myself?" he asked aloud wanting to listen to his own voice again. *Anything to help me stay sane,* he thought.

"I am a fool," he cried aloud, bringing his bound hands to his mouth. The fools had bound his hands in front, possibly to save themselves some work. The bonds were of papyrus twine and though his lips were already raw from chewing the hole in the sack, he bit the twine with renewed vigor. His thoughts reverted to the woman who was responsible for his current condition.

It was obvious that Khuit had done everything as per the plan that they had made together, everything except administering the antidote. She had gone to the embalmers who had promised to replace his body with a dead one for a consideration that had already exchanged hands. They had kept their word and handed his body over to Khuit, or he wouldn't be here. She could have avoided following through the whole plan. She had no need to go back to the embalming chamber and receive his body. After all, from her perspective, he had taken poison and without the antidote, he would have most certainly died.

Why?

Mentu stopped chewing.

Why did she go through the trouble of receiving his body from the embalmers, then binding his limbs and bundling him up in a sack, and throwing him here?

The answer came to him in a flash.

She did it because she wanted to be doubly sure that he was indeed dead. And she had another reason too. She had to do it because Sabaf, his friend who had arranged it all, would have become suspicious of her, if she hadn't. That wouldn't have helped, for Sabaf could have questioned the veracity of Mentu's will in front of the Will Executioner.

So she had taken his body from the embalmers, the body that she had thought belonged to a dead man, and thrown it here. Nobody would ever know, and after the burial was done, she would get his will executed.

But she couldn't have done it alone, he thought, chewing his bonds, spitting the fibers, and tasting the blood that was beginning to flow from his chafed gums.

Why did she do it?

He had loved her so much. He had risked his reputation and separated from his family, so that he could give her a respectable and safe life. He had taken her as his concubine, and he had done it because he thought that she had loved him back – if not with equal fervor and passion, at least with some respect and regard.

Mentu had reasons to believe that she cared. She had told him that with him dead, she too would not want to live, so after some very emotional moments, they had pulled themselves together, and Mentu had formulated a plan, in which Khuit had happily agreed to participate.

It was decided that after taking his body from the

embalmers, she would take him away to the village of Wahaq, where he would recover and then travel to South and disappear for three months. They would then meet in Nekhen, where Mentu would arrive with a new identity, and Khuit with the wealth that she would have inherited by getting his will executed. Mentu had earned enough to ensure a comfortable life for the two of them.

Had things gone according to plan, he wouldn't be here lying in this dark abyss, tasting his own blood, thirsty and hungry, and chewing the strong and hard papyrus ropes that she had used to bind his hands together.

He ignored the pain from his bleeding gums and his broken heart and continued to chew.

Suddenly, the string snapped. He wriggled his hands free and felt blood rush into his fingers. Awash with a new wave of optimism, he quickly untied his hands and tore through the sack, splitting it and freeing himself.

As he sat upon the dirt floor untying his feet, he tried to get his bearings. He was in a vertical shaft, which was a constricted space about a man's height in length and width. Stars twinkled outside the hole above, which appeared to be at quite a height. He wondered if the walls would have footholds that could let him climb up. He strained to hear the sounds. All he could hear was the air that rushed above and across the mouth of the shaft, whistling as it blew past.

A rat squeaked somewhere nearby. Mentu looked in the direction from where the sound came and saw two tiny red eyes staring at him. The rat reminded him of his hunger.

If only he could kill the rat…

Revulsion hit the back of his throat. He hated himself for thinking of eating a rat. He had never eaten one, and he wouldn't. Instead, he would escape. He had escaped one of the most closely monitored ceremonial mass-murder and he had outwitted his cunning concubine. He wasn't going to sit here and eat rats while she enjoyed his fortune.

It was night now. He decided that he couldn't do much until there was enough light.

"Perhaps it would be best to relax and recuperate. What do you think, my little friend?" he addressed the rat. The rat blinked and squeaked. It was clear that he was unhappy about his home being invaded.

"You'll have to bear with me for a few more hours," said Mentu, as he spread the sack upon the dirt floor and sat down upon it, leaning his back against the wall.

The moment he allowed himself to relax, memories flooded in once again. They came as random snatches from different times of his life.

He remembered his wife. He had moved to Abdju when he was eighteen and had been married for two years. He hadn't wanted to leave, but the King's summons had left him without recourse. He used to own and manage a small inn on the outskirts of Thinis, The inn was popular for its food and so for its cook – and when the King's Chief Royal Cook had heard of his culinary skills, he had offered him a job in the king's kitchen.

He had thought about it, long and hard, and then accepted the offer. His wife had cried. She had entreated him to refuse and stay, but he hadn't listened. They had a son then, and he wanted to provide well for him. The royal cooks were paid handsomely – in grain, in *heqt,* in linen, and in land. Today he owned land in five different cities. He even employed a scribe who did his revenues and taxes. Each year, he had grown in stature, until his mentor had died. Before his death, he had chosen Mentu as his successor, who had then become the Chief Royal Cook himself.

But being the King's favorite cook had its underside. He had to remain in Abdju almost the whole year. Only twice every year, he was allowed leave to visit his family in Thinis. In the beginning, his visits were welcomed by his family. His wife was happy to receive him in her bed and they made love with passion. But when his wife had realized that he would only be home to seed her belly and leave for the rest of the year, she had started to change.

Four children later, she had lain in his arms and told him that she didn't want another child. Her statement had shocked him.

"Why?" he had asked. "We can provide for them. I'm still rising in King's favors. Children are the gift of *Hathor*. They are the blessings of *Isis*. Why must we refuse to be blessed?"

"Ipy's wife died a month before you arrived," she said.

Ipy was their neighbor – a trader of beads. He wasn't as rich as Mentu, but he had done fairly well.

"That must be hard on Ipy," he had observed. Then thinking of how difficult it must be for the man to care for his five children, he had added, "He must marry again."

"You didn't ask how his wife died," Mentu's wife had fumed. "She died giving birth to his sixth child."

"That's sad. What happened to the child?" he asked.

"The child lived. With their mother dead, all the children, including the infant, are suffering. Ipy will marry again, I know, and have more children with his new wife. That would worsen their situation further – for no woman can love another's children the same as her own."

He had understood then. His wife was worried about dying and leaving her children behind.

"And for what and whom? For another piece of land and for a husband who is seldom home? Your own children think of you as a stranger who comes home only to bed their mother. Mentu, I don't want to become pregnant again."

That was the last time she had allowed him in her bed. Whenever he went home, they slept in the same room, but in different beds – and at that time Mentu was barely twenty-eight. His body needed succor. It needed to feel the warmth and softness of another body against it. His passion sought release.

So he had begun to seek release elsewhere - in Abdju's houses of love, in the streets of Ineb-hedj, and even in the wharves of the delta, where he would go to procure the meat of exotic animals, usually imported from Sinai and the lands beyond.

Khuit was a wharf wench, whose stories were shared by sailors and traders alike. She was beautiful enough to be a goddess, and a goddess she was – artful in lovemaking, creative in her methods, yet available at a price he could afford.

Mentu had met her three years after being thrown out of his wife's bed. In those three years, he had sampled them all. Big, small, thin, plump, obese, even skeletal; dirty, ragged, smelly, clean, happy, angry, bland, interesting, quiet, talkative – all forms and all kinds. Going to them was his way of finding solace, for there was nothing left to inspire him. Especially, since he made it to the seven favorites – the King's servants in the afterlife, because each morning he would rise to pray for the health of his King and to ward off the inevitable. As the King merrily ate and drank himself to his tomb, Mentu tried to lose himself in the quest of that momentary bliss, the glimpse of which he saw at the end of his trysts.

He didn't care who he threw himself upon and into, until he met Khuit, and then he had suddenly wanted to live again. He didn't care whether it would be a year or two, or ten, before the King died and swept them all along into his tomb. After finding Khuit, he had once again wanted to fill his remaining days and years with life.

So after spending three whole days and nights, and a substantial part of his earnings of the year, he had emerged from Khuit's embrace, sated and happy, and then he had asked her if she would like to come to Abdju with him.

He still remembered how she had looked then. Her golden hair fanned out upon the pillow sparkling in the sunlight that caught the edges of its strands, her beautiful fair complexion with a hint of rose in her cheeks, her long lashes half hiding her blue-green irises, a nose with a soft round tip, and lips that looked like rose-petals. She made him feel like a new man.

"Yes," she had replied, and his world had changed forever.

"But there will be no marriage," he had told her.

"I understand," she had said, "I don't expect men to leave their families for me. I shall be happy being your concubine."

Since then, his life had been beautiful. He had worked hard and tried not to think of his impending death, and then in the evening he returned to his rooms to find her waiting for him. It was amazing how she continued to look beautiful day after day, and how she could ignore his own signs of aging. His graying hair, his wrinkling skin, and his weakening teeth, he could feel their presence, but she saw past them.

She was the reason why he had found the courage to defy death.
She was the one who was responsible for his being in this hole.

∿∿ ◊◊◊ ∿∿

In Abdju, the royal mourning had been announced. Khuit found herself wondering how mourning and celebration could happen at the same time, for nearly the same reason. If King Djer hadn't died, his successor Djet wouldn't have become King. Among the royals, mourning was often pregnant with celebration. A King had to die for another King to be born.

Khuit found it disconcerting, but she was an intelligent woman, who some called cunning. She knew that it was akin to her own life – for if Mentu hadn't died, she would not inherit his wealth.

Death was necessary for life.

One only had to know how to use death.

It was the day after they had taken the bodies away to the embalmers. The mud-brick tomb that would receive the body of King Djer was constructed in his lifetime. Now, after his death, it was being prepared to receive not just his body, but also the bodies of those who shall continue to serve the King in his afterlife.

She sat looking out of the window of the living room in Mentu's quarters. Outside in the courtyard, she could see the relatives of others who had been sacrificed. Mentu's own family had decided to stay in an inn in the city. They didn't want to meet her, which was only natural. She wasn't insulted by it. She knew who she was, and though she wasn't proud of her past, she wasn't ashamed of it either. Mentu's wife, on the other hand, should have been ashamed. Had she not kept Mentu from her bed, he wouldn't have found Khuit. Khuit hadn't replaced Mentu's wife. She had merely filled a place that had been vacant for three years.

Khuit didn't begrudge the riches that King Djet would be showering upon Mentu's family. All that was theirs by right.

She didn't have the same right nor had she ever desired it. When Mentu had made her the offer to be his concubine, he had told her about Pharaoh Djer's failing health, and told her that he was destined to accompany Pharaoh into his tomb. *Three...at the most five years* was what he had said then. She had agreed in the hope that in five years time, she would win her freedom back.

First, Pharaoh Djer had lingered on.

She had prayed to *Osiris* for his early demise. When finally her prayers were answered, Mentu had changed his mind. He didn't want to die. He wanted to live into his dotage, sucking her remaining youth dry.

That wasn't nice of him.

Khuit remembered her first meeting with Mentu. She was displaying her attractive wares near an inn on the wharf where a ship had just docked. It was the time of business for the wharf wenches, for the sailors and the traders who hadn't seen the inside of a woman's thigh for weeks if not months, were usually easiest to pick as they clambered down the ships.

Mentu hadn't arrived on that ship. He was in the city shopping for exotic meat for the royal kitchen, and he spent his evenings raiding the wharves to satisfy his carnal desires. When she had first seen him, he wore a rather expensive pectoral and had a fine linen shawl wrapped around his shoulders. Her attention was drawn to him, because he was the best-dressed man on the wharf that evening.

He had looked at her and then he hadn't looked away. She liked it when men were drawn to her like that – moth to flame, man to woman – with no concern for another soul. She knew she was beautiful, but she also realized that she was almost at the end of her tether. Life as a wharf wench was agonizingly short-lived for most because each night they risked serving men who were short-tempered and violent. One of the girls had to retire when she was barely twenty-two and at the prime of her career, because her customer hadn't had the courtesy to spare her face when he was beating her mercilessly, trying to make his flagging staff rise.

After a wild night, the next morning, Mentu had told her about himself. He was the Chief Royal Cook of King Djer, and he was frightened of the day he would have to follow the King into the afterlife.

"He can die any day - today, a week or a month from now, or in a few years. Each morning, when I wake up, I pray to the gods for his long life, and then when the day ends, I go to bed in dread. I've been dying every day, but you fill my heart with hope. I know that I have to die. The King is morbidly obese. Each day his body grows in girth but slows in gait. His heart beats faster than the wings of a humming bird when he has to walk across the room. He will die soon – in a few years – three, maybe five. We will die along – we, the seven chosen ones, and all those whose names would come up in the last-moment lottery. Sometimes we envy the others – the ones who would have to live with the knowledge of their impending death only for a few moments. If you come with me to Abdju, I'll live each day between now and then. I'll leave you rich, I promise you that."

She had reviewed his proposal and accepted.

And then she had waited for the day to arrive. The King had lived on. Either through the sheer power of his will or through divine intervention, he tottered on, year after year. For ten years, King Djer had clung to life, and for ten years, Mentu had clung to her.

When the King had finally given up, Khuit had visited the temple of Osiris and offered him her own blood. She had prayed that Osiris would take King Djer away this time, and Osiris had heard her prayers.

And then that fool Mentu had changed his mind.

That son of a donkey had begun to think with his stele, which was natural, for it was a lot bigger than his heart. He had made a plan to cheat his King and to cheat her! That blundering fool, the mad nymphomaniac, had shared his plans with her and sought her help.

"Khuit, you must help me," he had come whining to her.

"Khuit, I want to live. I want to spend my life with you," he had begged.

Khuit had to agree, or he would have left her destitute. What else could she have done? The ten years that she had given to him, he had to pay for those, but he wasn't willing to.

All she did was help him keep his promise to her.

Now she was free of all encumbrances. She was still

young and with Mentu lying tied in a sack at the bottom of that dead hole, she was free. She stood up, letting her blue linen dress fall down in neat pleats. Her bare breasts that were still a few years from sagging, stood proud and majestic above the gathers of her dress. Her hair was beaded with red, yellow, and green stones, and her eyes were enhanced with the deepest shade of black on its edges and soft green upon the lashes. She looked beautiful and she knew it.

A smile played on her lips as she slipped her blue lily pendant upon her gold chain. The pendant was a relic from her old days on the wharf and it made her feel attractive and desirable.

She was now free once again, to feel desire.

She had felt it, six months ago. The King had become bed-ridden and given her a reason to dream. Everyone knew that the King was going to die soon. Some were distressed, for they were marked to follow the King into his tomb, some others were anxious and frightened, because they knew that their names would be in the lottery on the day of King's ascension into afterlife, but like Khuit, there were some others too, who were hiding their happiness, holding it close to their chests, for they were unhappy with their lives. She was one of those – she was waiting to start a new life, but she had to hide her hope and happiness in her bosom, never letting it light up her face or put a bounce in her step.

And she wasn't ready to let Mentu destroy it all.

So she did what she thought was right.

Now all she had to do was wait until the burial. Then she would start a new life.

〰 𓏥 〰

The rat nibbled at his toe. At first he felt ticklish, then

reality flashed and made him jump out his skin. The rat scuttled. Mentu touched his toe and discovered that the rat had chewed away some of the skin that had hardened around his toe. Its teeth hadn't broken through and there was no blood. He felt relieved for he didn't want the additional discomfort of a bleeding toe when he attempted to climb out of this dirty hole forsaken by the gods.

Rats, he thought, *were useless vermin.* They brought no happiness to anyone. If he ate one, the world would have one less to contend with.

He shook his head. Rats were unclean, as were pigs. They were not to be eaten. He was thinking with his stomach. His hips had gone numb from sitting in the same position for hours, so he moved his legs to tuck them beneath him, letting the weight shift from his hips to his feet. Under him was the brown sack, spread upon a dark ground.

With a start he realized that the day was beginning to dawn. He looked up. The sequined circle that hung overhead was no longer black, and the stars had almost disappeared. Soon it would be morning.

He got to his feet. Blood rushed into his veins causing his legs to tingle. The sensation didn't bother him. Instead it made him feel alive. Mentu looked around. He was right about the dimensions of the hole. Unfortunately, the walls were smoother than he had expected them to be. The first foothold he could see, a rock jutting out of the wall, was at eyelevel and he had nothing that he could use to reach it.

He looked around for a possible prop. The floor of the shaft was littered with leaves and bird droppings, the pungent smell of which had kept him sane during the night. A broken branch about a cubit long and as thick as his thumb had fallen through the hole. Other than that, there was his precious tattered sack and the papyrus ropes that were used to bind his hands and feet.

As it became brighter, he began to see the details. If he could manage to reach the rock and put his foot upon it, there were other holds that would see him out. A crevice to wedge his foot, another rock that he could reach if he stretched a little, and the root of a tree that probably grew on the ground outside the hole. His eyes stopped at the root. It was as thick as his arm and looked like it could possibly take his weight without snapping. Standing in the middle of the shaft and analyzing the details, he felt optimistic about his escape.

If he only had a rope that he could hook into the loop that the root made, he could safely haul himself out.

A rope, he thought. *Where can I find a rope?*

He looked at his *shenti*. It was strong new linen. It didn't matter if he scramble out naked, as long as he was alive. Excited at the prospect of escape, he unwrapped his *shenti* and split it in the middle lengthwise. Then he tied it with the sack using a tight double knot, the kind he had seen the fishermen make. That gave him another three cubit. He loosened a stone from the floor and tied it to one end of the ragged looking rope he had created, and threw it up.

He missed on his first try. He had expected to miss. The missile he had made fell about a cubit short of its target. He kept trying, ignoring the pain in his shoulder and the thirst that burned his throat.

After an hour, his arm aching from the exertion, he slipped down only vaguely conscious of his naked bottom coming in contact with the damp dirt.

"I can't do it," he whispered, tears stinging at the corners of his eye.

He sat there, feeling the pain in his arm, wondering whether it would have been better had he not seen Khuit smile in the mirror. He had worked in the royal kitchen all his life, and he had no experience of climbing out of such godforsaken holes.

Did I escape a death of glory only so that I could die in this hole, alone and naked? He asked himself as he lamented his piteous condition.

Then he remembered the rat that had nibbled at his toe the previous night and thought how terrifying it would be when starved and weak he would not have the energy to frighten the rat away.

It would eat me slowly. First, it will break my skin and drink my blood. The smell of my blood will then draw others of its kind, who would fight over my weak body. They would savor my body, devour it slowly, as I shall twist and turn in pain and agony, they would eat my nose, my eyes, my...

The gruesome imagery shook him out of his stupor.

The sky above was now a lovely clear shade of azure. It looked beautiful. He couldn't allow himself to die here and give up the many lovely years he could still spend in the world.

That scheming, conniving witch! I won't let her enjoy my property while my body rots here, leaving my ka alone to wander about with no body to go back to.

He stood up.

"*O' Horus, O' Sweet Isis*, help me," he prayed as he threw the rope up once again.

He watched as the rope undulated upward then rising above the root, it slowed and swung back as the stone ballast reached his height and fell through the loop of the root. The stone came rushing down, pulling the rope through the loop. Mentu thanked his gods and made the knot.

He was going to get out alive and then seek answers. He would go to his friend Sabaf who now remained the only person he could trust.

It wasn't yet evening when a naked man covered in dirt scrambled out of a hole. The place was deserted, but the bend in Nile told him where he was. He knew and trusted the river well. He would follow it North and find what he sought.

∿∿ 𓏤𓏤𓏤 ∿∿

The litter arrived at the entrance of the inn just a few moments after Mentu had.

He had stolen a *shenti* that was hung to dry behind a hutment. Clad in the threadbare *shenti*, his eyes devoid of kohl and his chest and arms of even the most basic ornaments, he would have looked like a beggar, had he not washed the dirt out of his pores and cleaned himself.

She, on the other hand, alighted from her litter looking beautiful and rich. She wore the blue linen wrap that he had bought for her last year. Her skin, damp from perspiration twinkled provocatively in the last rays of the evening sun. Around her neck she wore the same blue lily pendant that had snitched upon her the previous night. As she walked into the inn, he felt a sharp barb twisting inside his heart. He couldn't help but notice how young she still looked…*and how beautiful.*

As she disappeared inside, his senses returned.

He was here to meet his friend and seek his help.

But why was Khuit here?

He wondered as suspicion grew in his heart, clawing its way into its core.

He followed her in, avoiding the usher, for if their eyes met, he would recognize him instantly, and in all probability scream that he had seen a ghost, for the entire Egypt knew that at this time, he was dead and being eviscerated upon an embalmer's table.

Fortunately, another prospective guest had appeared behind him, and engaged the usher's attention.

Mentu knew this inn like the back of his palm. This was where he had learned about the pleasures of flesh. Sabaf, his friend of twenty years, was the owner of the inn. He was the man who had helped him arrange the exchange of his body at the embalmers. Now, Mentu's heart that beat hard against his ribs, wanted him to question Sabaf's friendship. For if everything was aboveboard, why was his concubine here?

His heart knew the answer, but it sought confirmation. Mentu found his way to the inner courtyard, which was Sabaf's personal domain. It was where he lived and kept his harem. Sabaf had concubines from the whole known world, but he had never married.

"What about children?" he had asked his friend many years ago.

"What about them?" Sabaf had shot back.

"Don't you want children? Someone you could leave all your wealth to?" he had asked.

His friend had laughed heartily.

"Do you think that's a good reason to have children?" he asked. "They drain you with their demands. You keep pouring your wealth down their greedy gut, because you feel responsible for their wellbeing. Their mothers hold you hostage through them, because they know that through their children, they can make you provide for them – because after a time, they turn into ugly loveless leeches that stick to you, drinking your blood, weakening you and making you squirm…"

At that time, having been spurned by his own wife, Mentu had agreed with his friends' assessment of wives, but not of children.

"I'm happy to be among friends and concubines. Friends are good for my heart, and my concubines take care of my body. I wouldn't let women into my secrets. I wouldn't trust them with my life, but I would trust you with it, my friend," Sabaf had told him then.

Today, moving through the same inn stealthily, he reflected upon Sabaf's words. He had trusted Sabaf and he had also trusted Khuit.

Had he been wrong in trusting them both?

As he stepped inside his friend's quarters, he got his answer. He moved stealthily through the antechamber, which was overly cluttered with statues of women laboriously carved so that they looked lifelike. Upon reaching the window that opened into Sabaf's bedchamber, he stopped and peeked inside. He recognized the chamber and the arrangement of the bed inside, for he himself had made use of it in past. The busts behind him had camouflaged Mentu, and he knew that if he didn't make a sudden move, they would never be alerted of his presence.

In the cool interiors of Sabaf's bedchamber, he could make out their silhouettes. They were confident and happy in the knowledge that Mentu was dead, so they had no reason to keep their voices low. The gaiety that rode their voices was enough to make him turn and leave, but a strange, masochistic desire kept him rooted to his spot, forcing him to watch. He knew what he would see, but he wanted to watch it all, so that he could burn those last run-down traces of love that he felt for her.

She sat in Sabaf's lap with her arms around his neck.

"Thank you," she said kissing him.

"Remember your promise," Sabaf said, his voice ragged, belying his rising passion.

"I remember everything, but now isn't the time to compare our lists. The will shall not be executed until after the burial," she told him, rising from his lap, letting his ready passion spring to attention. Sabaf held her hand and pulled her back.

"No," she whispered, extricating her hand from his. She walked away from him seductively. The way she would, when she was with Mentu. He knew her routine, and he knew how devastatingly exciting it could become, but today, it made her look like a lowbred woman…like the wharf wench that she was.

Still he couldn't tear his eyes away.

She backed away, slowly. Her hips moved provocatively under the blue linen of her tunic. Her breasts bounced softly, making her pink buds rise and fall rhythmically. Her soft, round belly with her deep mysterious belly button shook from her movement and made Sabaf groan softly.

First, she removed her wig, letting her natural hair fall free upon her shoulders. Then she slipped away her armlets.

Now she will move her right hand below her left breast and unhook her tunic, he thought.

The tunic slid down her body and dropped into a fluid blue heap on the floor. There she stood, in all her glory, naked except for her thong and the blue lily pendant.

Despite the disgust he felt for her, Mentu felt his own excitement rising. Inside the bedchamber, Sabaf was finding it difficult to contain his rising passion. "Remove that too," he said, his voice hoarse and rasping.

She will ask you to do it. Idiot, this is a game she plays with every man, thought Mentu feverishly.

"You do it," she said, her voice honey sweet, melodious as the soft cooing of a cuckoo.

Sabaf had been waiting for it, for he sprang up and tore away her thong. Then he wrapped his arms around her and pulled her to the bed, pushing her down upon it. The window between the bedchamber and the dark room, in which Mentu stood, was at the side of the bed where she lay now with her legs spread. The blue lily pendant glimmered lustrously between her breasts. Mentu was between her legs, his stele jutting out and glistening with need and pride. As he held it in his hand, Sabaf reminded Mentu of the statue of *Min*, the god of virility who was depicted with his erect member in his left hand, holding a flail in his right.

Suddenly Sabaf swooped down and tore the blue lily pendant away from her neck. The suddenness of his movement shocked Mentu, who wondered whether his friend had finally succumbed to Khuit's charms, for why would he concern himself with a woman's trinkets otherwise.

"You will never wear that again," he told her, his eyes riveted to hers, his anger coursing through him, stiffening him further, as he flung the pendant across the room, through the dark window, beyond which Mentu stood.

He is in love with her, Mentu thought as he bent to pick up the discarded pendant.

He heard her laughter.

Don't let her fool you, he wanted to tell Sabaf, *she cannot change – the blue lily is seared in her heart. The evenings she spent on the wharves are sewn in her soul.*

He looked at them one last time, attached through the madness called desire. Pushing, pulling, huffing, panting – the muscles of his hips tightening and loosening; moaning, groaning, rising, and falling – her soft silky thighs opening and closing, he saw them as they were, mindless animals fornicating only because their bodies demanded it.

He was that animal once, and his leash was in her hands. *But no more.*

ᴧᴧᴧ ∏∏∏ ᴧᴧᴧ

Three days after the burial, the Will Executioner's office had opened its doors once again.

Khuit arrived there in a curtained litter. She had no cause to hurry, for the ferry that she had booked herself on, left a week after.

When she walked in, wearing a honey-colored robe, her shoulders naked but painted in greens, blues, and yellows, she knew that all eyes would be upon her.

Unfortunately, she wasn't wearing her lucky pendant today, but it didn't matter. The blight upon her life, that miserable coward Mentu had been gone for a whole month, and her life since had been on the upswing.

Perhaps, her blue lily pendant wasn't so lucky after all.

She reached the Will Executioner's chamber and curtsied. The bored but harmless looking man waved her into a seat opposite to him.

"Yes?" he asked.

"Mentu, the Chief Royal Cook who was buried along with King Djer, may the gods rest his soul in peace, left me this will," she said, handing over the papyrus scroll to the Will Executioner as she settled down upon the bench in front of his table.

The Will Executioner looked perplexed.

Naturally, she thought. *After all, he doesn't know who I am.*

"I apologize for not introducing myself. I was Mentu's concubine for ten years. I lived with him..." she started.

"I know who you are," the Will Executioner replied. "But there is an issue."

"What issue? I have his will here. He made it two months before the *Awakening*," she asked with concern. There could be no problem with the will. The scribe who had written it out had read it aloud to her before Mentu had added his hieroglyph to the bottom of the scroll.

"He made another will a month before his glorious ascent to afterlife," replied the Will Executioner, tapping his writing pen upon another scroll that lay amongst many other similar scrolls on his table.

"What?" she asked, the world crashing around her. "This isn't possible. He wouldn't do this to me," she countered, her voice caught in a sob.

"He willed all his property to his brother," he told her, clearly concerned with the plight of such a beautiful woman.

"His brother? He didn't have a brother," she stuttered, shocked.

"Oh, he had a brother. His twin, who traveled all the way from Thinis to be here this morning, and he brought the will along. I can show it to you," said the man, touching the knob of his nose and rubbing it.

She wanted to ask him to stop doing that. She didn't like it when people touched their faces, especially their noses. Oddly she hadn't noticed until then that the Will Executioner had an extremely large and bulbous nose, and his skin was pitted and scarred.

He looked obnoxious.

She watched as the man rummaged through the rolls that lay upon his desk, making some of them fall to the floor.

"Yes, yes. It's here. You see? This is the will that has already been executed," he said, unrolling a scroll upon the desk and patting it down for her to see.

She sat there for many long moments, staring at the papyrus roll. It was the same as hers, and she recognized the hieroglyph of Mentu's name drawn in his hand, but the Executioner said that it was made in the name of his brother. *How could it be?*

Then, abruptly, she lost her calm and broke down.

The Will Executioner looked around helplessly, and then decided that a tumbler of water would be the right thing to offer to her. She took it from him, gracefully. Then sniffling, she asked him.

"So he left me nothing? For all those years that I slaved for him, I get nothing?"

"Ah, no," said the man, visibly relieved to see that the woman had regained her composure. "He did leave you something," he said.

"What?" she asked. *Perhaps there still was hope.*

The man pushed a small bundle made of rough linen, the kind they used for making sacks, tied with a piece of papyrus rope. The linen and the rope both looked dirty.

"What is this?" she asked.

"I don't know what is in it, but he left this for you," replied the Executioner, his own eyes popping out with curiosity.

Khuit pulled the little bundle toward her, and began untying it, her fingers trembling and her heart bouncing against her ribcage.

Inside lay her precious charm, her lucky blue lily pendant - the one that she had worn when she had gone to meet Sabaf.

She stood shaking for a very long time. Then, her voice aquiver with an ungodly supernatural fear, she asked, "who left this for me?"

"The twin brother," said the Will Executioner. "He asked me to give it to you when you came."

〜 ᑫᑫᑫ 〜

Historical Notes:

Between 3100 BC and 3500 BC, retainer sacrifices were carried out in Ancient Egypt.

Historians have discovered subsidiary graves in and around the tombs of the Kings of the first dynasty.

Historians are of the opinion that five hundred and eighty men and women were buried along with King Djer who was the son of King Hor-Aha.

The five Kings who are associated with retainer sacrifices are: King Hor-Aha, King Djer, King Djet, King Den, and King Qaa.

It is believed that the sacrifices were carried out either by poisoning the men and women who were marked to be buried alongside the King, or by strangulating them.

King Djer ruled from Abydos, which was then known as Abdju.

In ancient times, Memphis was known as Ineb-hedj.

Also by S.R. Anand

MYSTERIOUS KEMET - Book I
INTRIGUE AND DRAMA
IN ANCIENT EGYPT

Now available on Amazon
https://www.amazon.com/dp/1520568150

In this Collection, read...

I

A PRAYER TO OSIRIS

~ | First Intermediate Period | ~

Intef wishes to be Pharaoh, and he would be, if it weren't for his niece Neferu and nephew Mentuhotep. The only way he can win this game of political senet is by winning Neferu's heart and marrying her. But before he can accomplish any of it, Osiris must answer his prayers. What he doesn't expect is that Osiris might give him exactly what he asks for.

II

IMHOTEP'S SECRET DRAWER

~ | Old Kingdom | ~

Disturbed by the inexplicable disappearance of someone he secretly loves, Imhotep, the architect and builder of the Step Pyramid, opens the hidden compartment in his work desk and finds something shocking. Left with a gruesome memento, Imhotep must learn a terrible truth about the woman he desires and accept the consequences.

III

THE PHAROAH'S EAR

~ | New Kingdom – Amarna Period | ~

Sunamun, a junior sculptor in Thutmose's workshop, is enamored by the beauty of Queen Nefertiti. When he stumbles upon a secret rendezvous between Thutmose and a mystery woman, he is pulled into witnessing and assisting the power struggle following the death of Akhenaten, which eventually leads him to discover two truths that he must never tell.

IV

SAVIOR OF EDFU

~ | First Intermediate Period | ~

When his lost love beckons, Ankhtifi, the nomarch of Nekhen sees an opportunity in Edfu, which neglected by its nomarch Khuy, has fallen into poverty and anarchy. An elaborate plan, carefully woven into the carnal adventures of Khuy and his mad brother, is executed with finesse. The plan begets its goal and Edfu is saved, but Edfu's gain turns out to be Ankhtifi's loss.

V
THE KEEPER OF SECRETS
~ | New Kingdom | ~

Anen, an artist who works at the building site of Djeser Djeseru is the favorite pupil of Senenmut, the Master builder. He is also the secret lover of Senenmut's mistress. As he toils over the relief of the Punt expedition and prepares himself for the visit of Pharaoh Hatshepsut, a mysterious man turns his life upside down.

∿ | ⵊⵊⵊ | ∿

MYSTERIOUS KEMET - Book I
Intrigue and Drama
in Ancient Egypt

Now available on Amazon
https://www.amazon.com/dp/1520568150

TOGGLED

TOGGLED is a dark psychological thriller, which explores the deepest recesses of the schizophrenic mind, as it takes you from a modern day suburban neighborhood into the streets of Ancient Egypt, and then brings you back to a grim and dangerous place where death is real, but murder isn't.

Toggled...is the mind of Brice Ward.

TOGGLED on Amazon
https://www.amazon.com/dp/B06XW9KMKK

ARRIVING SOON…

MYSTERIOUS KEMET - Book III
PASSION & BETRAYAL IN ANCIENT EGYPT

For Updates on Pre-Order & Release
please follow the author on:

FACEBOOK: *https://facebook.com/SRAnandAuthor*
TWITTER: *https://twitter.com/SRAnandAuthor*
AMAZON: *https://amazon.com/author/sranand*

A NOTE OF THANKS

Dear Reader,

I'd like to thank you for reading "Mysterious Kemet - Book II." If you enjoyed reading it, please review it on Amazon. I shall be thankful for your kind gesture.

I've tried my best to ensure that this book doesn't contain those pesky typographical errors, yet perfection has never been my forte, so if you chance upon any, please let me know, and I'll try to correct it as soon as I can.

I would love to hear from you at *SRAnand.Author@gmail.com*.

Thanks once again.

ABOUT THE AUTHOR

S.R. Anand is a storyteller who writes historical and psychological thrillers, epic fantasy, and science fiction. When she is home, she can be found in her room, scribbling, typing, and guzzling tea; smiling at her invisible characters and driving her family up the wall.

When she isn't writing, she daydreams and finds herself transported to alternate worlds – historical, fantastical, or dystopian. She cannot usually stop herself from reading stories in the events happening around her and telling them, but whenever she can pull the brakes, she draws, paints, and teaches.

Her Facebook page is *facebook.com/SRAnandAuthor* and her Twitter handle is *@SRAnandAuthor*.